THE RESTORER OF THE BREACH

Finding Hope and Healing on the Edge of Despair

Darla L. Gooden

authorHOUSE®

AuthorHouse™
1663 Liberty Drive
Bloomington, IN 47403
www.authorhouse.com
Phone: 1-800-839-8640

First published by AuthorHouse   5/4/2010

ISBN: 978-1-4490-7510-1 (e)
ISBN: 978-1-4490-7511-8 (sc)
ISBN: 978-1-4490-7512-5 (hc)

Library of Congress Control Number: 2010900460

Printed in the United States of America
Bloomington, Indiana

This book is printed on acid-free paper.

This book is dedicated to my beautiful children:

Kenneth Jr.
Joshua
Jeremie
Kristen
Alexis
Terrance

Thank you for your timeless, unconditional love.

Acknowledgements

I WOULD LIKE TO HUMBLY ACKNOWLEDGE MY mother Bessie, who taught me unconditional love; my father James, who taught me discipline; my siblings, Bunny, James, Catrina, Eric and William, whom I love dearly; and my children, Kenneth Jr., Joshua, Jeremie, Kristen, Alexis and Terrance, for whom I live my life for.

I'm truly blessed and duly grateful to publish my first book. As such, I would like to extend my profound gratitude to Annie L. Chiles – creative writer; Dee Dee Woods – photographer; Genel Burwell – editor; and Genese Williams – artist and Maura Ackley – cover design. God supplies my every need and this book would not be possible if not for these people. I am forever indebted to each of you.

I wish to express my deep affection and appreciation to my church family and Pastor R. Douglas and Lady Roslyn Chukwuemeka of New Destiny Christian Church.

I would like to pay tribute to the many people who have given freely of their time, their hearts and their resources to support this project. A partial list includes: Diane Walker, Fred Gammage, Onesimus Strachan, Tammy Lutz, Diane VanPatten, Chelsea Faliveno, Stephanie Skinner, Horace & Lavera Bell, Katherine Robinson, Debra Rhone, Corey Walker, Patrick Melvin, Kiyyah Walker, Winona Jackson, Melissa Walton, Tony & Angel Rochet, Linda Gammage, Jackie Gooden and Stan Kukucka.

Finally, I'm thankful for the bookstores, booksellers, book clubs and all readers who support this book and my cause. Thank you from the bottom of my grateful and blessed heart.

The Restorer of the Breach

Prologue

Have you ever noticed how you can be sitting in the busiest places and find stillness? Stillness doesn't always usher in peace. Sometimes it is that eerie place that precedes disaster. It can be a place where you are isolated from the events going on around you. You are seated in the midst of it with "reserved seating" stamped on your forehead. Isolation can be forced, like a cell, separating you from the actions and interactions of the events. Isolation can be a shield of protection, similar to those worn by ancient gladiators in the Roman Coliseum, protecting the heart from the blows of the opponent. I sat in the courtroom finding myself in this place of stillness, and I knew it wasn't the green pastures where spiritual restoration happens and peace abides. I was either trapped in a prison cell, or I was in the battle of my life. Either way, it was intense torment.

Silence isn't golden and what you don't know **can** hurt you, so throw out those old nuggets of wisdom and face the reality of today and its tarnished gold. Truth is piercing and the exposure to sudden light is blinding. Truth is in conflict with the great lie that "everything will be all right." Truth clashes with darkness, and the light that illuminates also blinds. Truth is not always what you want to hear, but, by necessity, truth is what you need to know.

Have you ever just sat in silence, screaming within, and realized no one wanted to be in that silence with you? Silence allows secrets to grow like mold in dark places behind the walls, in basements, climbing up the dark side of life ever growing and contaminating what it comes in contact with. Secrets have a hidden life of their own and must be sought after and dug up - like mushrooms, they don't go with everything. Secrets will grow even when they are not tenderly tended. When they are reluctantly and forcibly surrendered they cringe in the light, unable to focus because they have been held captive in darkness for so long. As a Christian I lived my life knowing truth is light and life and *men love darkness rather than the light, because their deeds were evil* (John 3:19b).

Disclosed or surrendered secrets provide no immediate freedom and there is not any great sense of relief or validation. Once darkness is dispelled, it is not like the curtain rising on your favorite play - there isn't a standing ovation. All you experience in this revelation of light is shock - squinting and tearing. You get to see close up how ugly and contemptible these hidden monsters are. They are out from under the bed and dispossessed from the closet and now they are bathed in the tears of the innocent and the regret of the unsuspecting. These secrets now isolate you from the world around you, drawing you into their web of intrigue and silence. You are now behind the wall where the mold is growing, or in the Coliseum in mid-battle.

So here in this courtroom I sit among people feeling lonely and longing for normality. I sit quite unaware of exactly what is being said and what all this movement around me is. Have I somehow fallen behind a veil of secrecy and invisibility in some covert operation with an espionage theme where, at the end, the hero walks away to theme music? Is the fat lady getting ready to sing, and am I in the audience of an amazing reality sitcom? At that moment I adjust my eyes and look up to see if it is time for the opening lines and the bailiff indicates we should all stand as the Honorable Judge enters the courtroom. He enters, like the conductor of a great symphony. Then reality jerks me back hard into the now of this darkness in the midst of daylight.

How did I get here, and what led me, Darla, to be sitting on the left side of the courtroom behind prosecutors who are the legal representatives of the state for my children? It is unimaginable to me that they would ever require legal representation. This case and this cause found me, and I have to see God, the Restorer, be victorious in it. This came into the safety of my home, snatched and tore my children from the safety of their beds and took them into a life they were unfamiliar with - stole their innocence and betrayed their confidence.

People have different reactions to the shock and tragedies that ambush and invade their lives. Real life is often *too* real, and response to what it demands of us is individual and different. It is the personal expression of pain that begins as a sharp breath - cutting, stabbing and transforming into a relentless throbbing, separating you from yesterday's tranquility and forcing you into today's reality. Some people desire to take charge of what they don't understand, thinking if they can just get on top it, interact or redirect it, then perhaps they can control the insanity and relieve their inability to have prevented it. It is almost as if they want to put up barriers to stop a tsunami or, at the very least, lay their boards on it and ride the waves of disaster to safer and dryer ground.

My children, my beloved children, have had the unimaginable happen to them. They have been molested, their innocence shattered and the *Big*

Nasty has come to our neighborhood and forced its way into our household uninvited. The screams of my children have not been heard because of the great silence surrounding them and swallowing their protests. Secrecy has clamped its nasty, sweaty hands over their mouths and their screams are trapped within them. They have been mangled in the insanity of predatory evil and as much as I hate the words, they have been stalked, seduced and made victims. My boys have been violated and no matter how I try, I can't wake up from this reality and label it a dream.

Either way, we are standing in the courtroom of the Honorable Judge awaiting the unfolding of the dishonorable events as we must stand up to give attention and reverence to the darkness and the silent screaming. The bitter taste of gall and rage fills my mouth again, and I know insanity is not the same as evil and no judgment can ever repay for what has been taken. So, in the midst of justice being served and in the process of prosecution and defense of what cannot be defended, I forced myself backward in time to again revisit the day that led to today's courthouse agenda.

Part I
ALL RISE!

One

My son came quietly into the room. This son is quite handsome, with great athletic ability. He is quiet, spirited, well-mannered and yet somewhat lazy when it comes to chores. It was too early for him to be home from school, which made my "mom ears" perk up. I remembered fussing about him missing practice, noting his eyes were red as if strained. He sat down in the chair like an elderly gentleman - weary of life. He looked pitiful as I began to rag on him about missing practice. His voice was very quiet and solemn as he said to me,

"Mom, I came home early because I need to talk to you about something important." I asked,

"What is it?" a bit impatiently.

"Mom," he said, "it is about someone you are close to."

Fearing this could be serious I sat down on the couch across from him and explained,

"When it comes to you and your brothers and sister, I am not close to anyone." my voice becoming solemn and quiet, matching his.

He breathed slowly with down cast eyes. Sitting for what seemed like an eternity, he just stared at me. Finally, he spoke,

"Well, I want you to know that our church youth worker has been molesting me."

I thought I was hearing wrong, or that I misunderstood what he said. I knew it couldn't be a joke because this would not be a topic for joking in our house. I needed him to repeat it, to say it again, and he did. I was still having difficulty hearing. It was then I wished for a nightmare and hoped someone would soon come and wake me. I really needed to wake up soon. You see, all truth doesn't come with great rejoicing - sometimes it is sad and solemn. This was truth and it was no dream. I then asked my son how long this had been going on - he responded for the past five years.

1

I am uncertain where I went at that moment. It was mind travel, a place outside reality where fear and rage live together. Somewhere on the slippery edge of the mainstream that borders insanity. It was a place void of stop signs or red or yellow caution lights, a place where collisions are eminent. I remember asking him if he was sure, that it was the church youth worker, as if hearing it again would somehow pull me back off the edge into a calmer place called yesterday. You see, my innocence, like his, was being shattered and the protective wall that I had built over the years was being breached without my permission.

As I looked into the eyes of my son, filled with fear and betrayal, I knew this was truth. Not the lovely, revealing and pure truth, but the now and nasty reality of actions taken against his will. He was drowning right there in my sight, and no matter what I felt, I had to give him a life jacket to prevent him from going further down into the nastiness that had engulfed his life. There was no time for me and my thoughts. He stood there in the shadows, limp and shaken, as if telling me had exhausted every bit of strength he had. I knew then that he needed the comfort and reinforcement of my love and understanding. Yet, how could I give understanding to what I could not even give definition? I thank God for Robo-Mom! Somewhere in me was his mother, pushing aside shock and fear, who began to walk over to my son and held on to him as tight as I could, telling him that I was so sorry that I didn't know any sooner. Regardless of what some people think, we live in an evil world and if you don't believe it just watch the news! Yet, this is the news that happens to other people. This happens to people who don't watch over their children, who entrust them to strangers. This happens to women who are weak, with even weaker morals - it certainly doesn't happen to good people. What a discovery, to find I could be awake and asleep at the same time. None of us are exempt from happenstance, and evil is always present while the devourer is always hungry. Bad things really do happen to good people. This is one of the hard lessons of life - it rains upon the just as well as the unjust, and when it rains we all need an umbrella because everyone can get soaked in an unexpected downpour.

My thoughts were a contradiction to the facts my son was presenting. No, he wasn't in some brutal, physical pain. That would actually have been easier. No, he wasn't physically injured in some way - cut or beaten by some stranger with even stranger intentions. That evil I could have understood. His abuser was a Christian husband and father who had been entrusted with the spiritual guidance of so many young people. I think this is when the word "betrayal" first began to form in my mind. The taste of it began to fill my mouth with a nauseating thickness and coating my tongue to pollute everything I said.

Betrayal is being delivered into the hands of an enemy in violation of your trust. It is deception at its highest level: to be led astray and deceived.

There is no real way of explaining what transpired next. There wasn't a manual to advise me of the steps to take or what to do in case of sexual abuse of my son and, if there was, I wasn't aware of it. It is the silent taboo that no one wants to talk about. Men don't want to speak about it, teachers don't teach it, preachers don't preach it. There isn't a paragraph in the weekly woman's journal between recipes and the gardening aids to explain how to handle this occurrence. One is left on their own, fumbling to figure out what to do next and who to call first. How was I to put words to what I couldn't even speak about without fear and pain?

I let go of him and found myself continuing to ask, "Are you sure?" as if he would not know what had happened to him. I didn't want to know the details, because that meant it was true and action was necessary. My eyes were searching his eyes and, with every look, reality was staring back at me. His eyes were searching mine to see if he was devalued in my eyes. He had been living in a danger zone - in a state of constant panic and fear. For years he existed in a place shrouded with secrets that he didn't know how to disclose. Someone violated him for their own pleasure without any thought of him. He was waking from a nightmare, and I was beginning to live in one. We were there together, standing like survivors and only our love was holding us together. My son had no words for what had happened to him, he was trying to make sense of it for my understanding, trying hard not to offend me.

Two

At first I really didn't understand how this could happen, or why my child did not tell me sooner. I was just as innocent as he was and I thought this was random and not intentional. It was probably some kind of misplaced touching that made my child uncomfortable. Surely it was something that I could deal with and control - it couldn't be molestation, and certainly not for five years. That would mean it began just before he began middle school. I was in a daze, and would be for a long time to come. Days went by before I realized I had not showered - the children reminded me that I needed to cook dinner. I drove past my route at work and did not even realize it for miles and miles. Before I knew it, I was on the phone calling the elder at my church and words that were disjointed began to come out of me. I was beyond tears and beyond sanity. It wasn't just confusion. I was, like my son, in shock and severe pain and needed help.

"Elder, I need to tell you something that's important. My son has told me that the church youth worker has been molesting him."

We all need someone in our turmoil. In the absence of reasoning we need the guy with the zappers - the true devil-busters to come in and eradicate the bad and bring in the good. That is what I was hoping for - someone to come in wearing a white hat who would take charge of the mess. You see, no one is really prepared for the *Big Nasty* because it really doesn't happen to good people, and it certainly doesn't happen to children. Yet, a brother, or even a sister, is born for adversity - to be there with you, even when they don't know what to do, either. They are more than hand-holders, they are people who will walk in the madness with you, unashamedly standing with you even when the world misunderstands and condemns you.

> *"A friend loveth at all times, and a brother is born for adversity."*
> *Proverbs 17:17*

The elder on the other end of the line seemed to take forever to understand what I was talking about. I was frustrated with her, not knowing that I wasn't connecting my thoughts, and my words were garbled and disjointed.

"Darla, I will be right there," she said.

She came with another sister, who was also a friend. They knew one thing for sure - that this situation sounded like either a woman in labor or a crime in action. Either way, the warning bell had gone off. The night seemed to go on forever when, in reality, it wasn't very long at all before my sisters in Christ appeared at the door. They came in silent and strong, joining me in tears yet supporting me and anchoring my son.

I began thinking about the passage of scripture in the Bible about David and the city of Ziklag - how they kidnapped David's wife and children. He came home to his city to find it had been invaded and burnt to the ground. How does this happen to a king? Where were the people who were close to him, and weren't they watching? Why would he allow his wives and children to be in jeopardy? What a comparison it was for me to look around my home and see what I had been building being destroyed, and that my children had been taken prisoner by someone who was an enemy dressed in sheep's clothes. How evil is evil; what do you do; and how do you handle this type of betrayal? Even David's men wanted to turn against him and desired to kill him. Who did I get to kill? Could I have this type of retribution also? Was it only for the King, or was it for the King's kids, also?

Invasion is the forced entry of someone into your personal place - it is trespassing to the highest degree. My treasures, like David's, were stolen away. The innocence of my child, his virtue and future, was in jeopardy. How was I to respond to this type of attack? As we sat at my dining room table the important questions began to be asked and the details began to come forth. Details that I didn't want to hear - the when and how and how long. It is more than my mind could hold.

As I listened to my sister's calm voice ask questions, a reassuring quietness of spirit moved in. We wept, all of us, with my son. We cried for losses that we could not even measure. Yet, we cried in hope. We held each other because we needed someone to hold on to so that we would not get carried away by this storm. We had to ask direct personal questions about what and when, and we staggered at the responses.

Three

Tears don't stop just because you run out of internal water and I have not stopped crying since the day this began. I cry for my children and for your children, who are not safe in a world of terrorists that are not on foreign soil or unfamiliar grounds. I cry for those who have not resolved what they endured, and I cry for their future. Tears are not a sign of weakness - they are how you maintain sanity in an insane world. You learn how to cry out unto The Restorer and to release the pain threatening to swallow your mind. Tears are a response to life, and pain is a reality of life. Tears give you empathy for those enduring hardships, now and in the future. We mourn with those who mourn and we cry because violence is in the land. The spirit of mourning has been released. The door has been left unlocked and evil has rushed in upon our children who are suffering great violations from those entrusted with their care.

It was at my table that my son arose to begin his journey to freedom and manhood. The final question the elder asked was,"What do you want us to do?" After all, didn't he have the right to make the decision since it happened to him, even though it was happening to me also as I relived the details with him? We went over the options as best as we knew them, not really knowing where to begin. My man-son responded in quiet firmness, "I want him to go to jail."

There are no Purple Hearts or Silver Stars given for children who make a stand against an enemy more powerful than they - the thief who comes and forcibly steals their innocence. Yet, he should have received a medal that night. Why? He refused to allow his assailant, a pedophile, victory over him any longer. We often think we have faced or seen real evil, but until that day, I had only seen the prelude and not the show.

You probably think that it was very easy to know where to start with something like this, but believe me; it wasn't easy at all because I was actually involved. Nothing is easy when your issue is so distasteful to many. The road map was not easy to read, and I was constantly questioning myself. I questioned myself because there might have been other people involved and the predator hadn't been apprehended yet. So I couldn't blast him, I couldn't have a public reaction and give him the opportunity to flee. He could have moved on like the transient spirit he was - to find new victims and a new operational base. Like David in the Scriptures, I couldn't shake what kept following me - I had to seek the right course of action. David called for the ephod to inquire of God; I also called for the wisdom of God, The Restorer.

How do you tell other family members that your son (their grandson or nephew) has been violated? What is it you can ever say to them to give them understanding of what has happened? How do you comfort them in the loss of their innocence and violation? How do you understand their anger when you are so filled with rage yourself? Who do you trust to tell, and who can put words and voice to this insanity? How do you keep all this silent so you can proceed to capture and incarcerate the real villain and help others understand you are not the villain? I had so many questions, so many explanations to everyone who, said under their breath, "somehow, through negligence, this must be your fault." How was I to protect my mind from the cloak of silence surrounding pedophilia? How was I to protect myself from accusations that would further push me past the brink of my own sanity?

There was someone always with me - a shadow of strength. Yet, I didn't know whether they were physical or spiritual. I was being upheld, but I just couldn't make out the images. I heard directions being given and followed them, hoping they were the voice of the **ONE** behind the ephod that David sought. I was preparing to shatter the silence surrounding the code and mask of pedophilia. I realize now that to do nothing only gives consent to evil. This code of silence would prove to be more extensive than I could have ever imagined. What my son and I wanted to believe was that this was an isolated incident. Reality was that this was just the beginning of a saga that would expand to other victims and bring out a history of continued and repeated acts of pedophilia.

Four

We decided to call our pastor - after all, the predator was a member of our local church and a worker among the youth. I let the elder speak to him and discuss in detail what my son and I had told her. He then cleared his calendar and immediately agreed to meet with us the next day at the church. The very first words I heard my pastor say to me was, "we need to get the authorities involved." Little did he know I only stopped by his office out of courtesy - I had already spoken to a friend of mine, an attorney, to find out how long I had to file charges. Our pastor has no toleration when it comes to violence against children, so I understood his position.

We were sitting across from one another in a steel-frame office evidencing shock and betrayal. We sat, my son, my pastor and I, reliving and listening to what we didn't even want to imagine or know. As my son spoke quietly and straightforwardly, words detailing what we never wanted to know, I realized he was acknowledging them for the first time. You see, he had been living in a city under siege by a manipulative and self-serving invader.

Once he began disclosing he couldn't stop telling the atrocities endured in his own private "Dachau". In this Herodian situation, the innocence of young boys was slain for the pleasure and purpose of unimaginable evil. In this 21st century genocidal camp, victims like my son were enslaved - the enslavement being relational. It was by threats and shame they were held hostage in silence. From the outside their lives appeared normal and those around them saw the predator as a great worker among children.

I felt the nausea building inside me, as a volcano about to erupt, and thought at any moment I would release the acid of fear, rage, and brokenness of soul and mind all over the purple couch. I saw the flexing jaw line of my pastor and quickly identified it as rage constrained. For a moment it was a comfort to have another who was suffering with me. His strained and angered, yet patient face, his quiet stern voice - these all confirmed more and more this wasn't a dream. He carefully allowed my son to speak freely, even though neither of us really wanted to hear what must be told. The duality of my being began to surface. I could measure the amount of emotion I released at any given time to maintain the sanity that would keep me from exploding prematurely.

We listened - we prayed - we cried, and then we needed a course of action. There was the whole process of reporting the crime and none of us knew quite where to begin. It wasn't because of ignorance, but because of shock. It was like a slow motion replay of a current event.

Strategy is important to the overthrowing of a tyrant. When you come against evil you can't throw miscellaneous items in his general direction hoping to hit him. Real evil is not like a video game - you can't keep trying until you complete a level and then move to the next. With real evil you may only get one good attempt before they slide behind the veil of secrecy to never be heard from again.

Five

My son and I left my pastor's office to go to the precinct with uncertainty. Driving there seemed to take forever. We reported to the police station in the middle of the night - my son, my mother, a friend and I expected to find a police sergeant behind a big desk awaiting our report of a crime, like on television. Instead we found a newly decorated office with a window, a counter, and staff who were not in uniform and who seemed surprised to see us there. You see, today very few people go to the station - they simply call the police. We never thought of calling them to our home, however. Again, we didn't know what to do - after all, this was an "after the fact" notification of a crime.

How do you answer the question, "What can I do for you?" Where do you begin to explain to a stranger what you want to report, and who it is, and where it happened and why? It was difficult to articulate to anyone. I tried to tell it all in one sentence, and it didn't make sense to me or the person I was talking to. They would simply say, "Okay, well just one moment." Didn't they know how long "one moment" could be? There was a lifetime of pain captured in that "one moment." Then, someone else appeared and I had to start all over again. God was there - His still, small voice spoke within me and I could not shut it down. How could I be impatient with those whom I needed to bring justice to my situation? So I started over speaking slower, hoping somehow I did not have to repeat it again.

This officer, however, gently led us into the disclosure with sensitivity. She spoke with quiet authority and assurance of her ability to address this. We somehow knew she would, in fact, pursue this for us. She helped me to understand the process of taking the report. My son and I followed her along down a long corridor that led to the room where all our secrets must again be disclosed. We breathed slowly as she gently guided us through what must be done. It was a procedure we needed to follow. It was unpleasant because facts void of feelings are cold and bitter realties that don't fit on a beautiful landscape canvas with poetic overtones. So all the bare facts were poured out to satisfy the requirements of the process, and finally we were released from any further disclosure on that night.

This process was only the taking of the report - no warrants had been issued, no real action taken. You see, like anything else, this process was time consuming and what happened is that I became defeated as everything seemed to take too long. The process, although necessary, was discouraging and I needed those around me to continue to push me to move forward. Once the report was filed, I met with another group of detectives to go to the next stage of making the arrest. We were doing the initial work and it was draining all the life out of us. In the past twenty-four hours I learned of the crime against my child, called for help, met with my pastor, and went to the precinct to report it.

All this in twenty four hours - and still I wasn't done because there was yet no arrest.

Six

I remember being in the courtroom and seeing him, the predator, sitting in a seat reserved for the defendant. It was the first time since all this began that I saw him - the man who had come into the life of my children with a badge of trust. How is it that he was afforded the privilege of being a defendant, as if there was anything he could defend? The ones who needed to be defended were the children, not the Pedophile.

This pedophile came into the lives of my children as a Christian worker, married, with a child of his own. The predator spoke with great commitment to the future of children. He didn't wear a raincoat, look like a pervert, or offer them candy. He was a father himself and only wanted to share with my children what they didn't receive from their own father. He gave them what is important to all children - his time, his energy, his encouragement, and faith. You see, pedophiles fill in the blanks. They have no distinguishing markings, except they love to be where children are. They are not suspicious looking or uneducated people. They can have degrees, be articulate, socially acceptable, respected members of society and not have a criminal background. What they do is done under the cover of secrecy, and even when they are discovered it is hidden because of shame and fear.

Our children have nothing to be ashamed of, yet because of our ignorance, they have much to fear. You see, they have been victimized and abused and they should not be hiding in closets as if they did something wrong. They need to see us as a family, a community rallying behind them to punish this injustice and victimization. They need to be vindicated and understood, not hidden behind some mask of propriety that only causes them to act out in later in life in response to what has been done to them. They need a hollering place where they can again learn to really cry about what they have been forced to endure.

This man was interested in what interested children, and he related to them at their level of understanding. He encouraged them in school, sports, and music. He was always available to them, just a phone call away. He was never too busy and spoke of the men they would one day become. He surrounded himself with children - both boys and girls. He was a big kid himself and likable. (The pedophile is a great actor and a chameleon that changes to fit the situation). He crept through the door left open to fill a vacant position in their lives and to help where he saw help was needed.

For instance, "Evangelist Darla, I know you are busy working. I am going down to the church, do your kids need a ride"?

Or, even while I was sitting at the table helping my kids with their homework, "Evangelist Darla, you seem overwhelmed. Can I help"?

He would say softly, with a quiet voice, "This is what real ministry is all about, helping others."

I often think that, as a single mom, when fathers aren't in their place, many things can go wrong. When they are too busy with careers or causes, predators will see children hungry for attention. Fathers provide protection, provision, and must be responsible. I have heard it said that fathers are like fences that surround a house providing protection. Without these "fences" Satan easily creeps right in and spoils the house. It is as hard to be a father as it is to be a mother - both require tremendous sacrifice. We both fill an important part in the life of our children because we balance them. We are the hedge surrounding and nourishing them so that they can grow strong and protected. Yet, the father provides identity to their children, he stands in the formation process as what they desire to become. When a father's identity is undesirable or absent, boys look for other examples of what they should be. Without wisdom they look for what appears to be a good and available example. As mothers we have much to offer our sons, but we cannot offer them what we have never been; we cannot offer them manhood. Boys are searching for true identity, and in a world of absenteeism it is hard for them to find out who they should become. Who will stand accountable to this generation of young men for their development? Who will help them turn their disappointments into fuel for success? Who is it that is supposed to stand and defend them from abuse and the abuser? The pedophile is looking for the weak link, the unprotected, the house without a fence and we have given them a wide range of choices.

Recalling the story of David and his men, what happened to David's watchmen and why wasn't adequate defense left behind? It was too much to be done alone, women couldn't handle all the decisions, pressures, development, and protection - men were needed. David realized our most valuable possessions are our families, and then one another. Unfortunately today's society doesn't place enough value on the family. We find so many of our children and women isolated, victimized, and open to abuse. As once a wife and now a single mom, I have sat in the seat of abuse and neglect for a big portion of my life.

I was married to a drug addict, my children's father. He chose drugs over our family and in doing so, he left us unprotected. He was the key that could lock out any potential abuser, but because of his own abuse, he was an ineffective protector.

In the courtroom, I looked over at the seat of the defendant and I was appalled that the one sitting there was the abuser and not the abused. I resented having to bring my child into this courtroom to face again this man who terrorized his life. He sat there as a defendant, looking normal, composed and forward; not back at the effects of his deeds. He was not in shackles or a prison uniform because his rights had to be protected and he had to receive a fair trial. The jury could not be adversely influenced. My intellect understood what my heart did not. I cried for my child who, even in the courtroom, continued to be victimized.

Seven

The Judge read the Indictment, "The state of Arizona charges the defendant with over thirty counts of sexual abuse against a minor." The room began to swim and blackness filled my eyes as I knew I had fainted. Quickly I realized that only happens in the movies - in real life you have to sit through the pain. I had to sit through the reading of the charges and know it was my child they were talking about. I had to listen to all of it and hear what I didn't want to hear.

My mind flashed back to the police report and I remember sitting and waiting for the detectives to call. You see, going to the precinct was just to initiate the process. At the precinct I received instructions to call the Child Agency to follow up the report.

My frustration for the process to apprehend the pedophile was beginning to show as I felt so overwhelmed. After all, to not alert him of our knowledge and risk fleeing, I had to appear normal. My elder friend told him not to call the children because of some issues we were having as a family. I prayed that he wouldn't become suspicious; telling him that would only work for a short period of time. I needed this to move faster - I was becoming anxious for his apprehension. I couldn't let him get away with what he had done. I knew my son deserved vindication and I wanted to provide him with the assurance that he was worth fighting for and this pedophile deserved punishment. My mind and emotions were moving so fast I could only hope I was doing and saying the right things so as to not further damage my son. As we returned home from the precinct my son began to open up more with details of what had happened to him. Details I didn't want to hear, but needed to hear and, more importantly, he needed to release so they would no longer have power or dominion over him.

I decided I really needed to discuss this again with my other children to make sure they understood what had happened to their brother so they would not call or communicate with this individual. I also needed to ask questions to make sure that they had not been molested too. Of course I was sure they had not been, but my mother's intuition kept pushing me. So I spoke with each of my other five children. I questioned their relationship and the times they were alone with him. Each one said nothing had happened to them and, believe me, I was relieved that only one of my children had been molested. Yet, something in me still continued to persist - pushing me toward a particular son. I hoped I was wrong, but I decided to speak to him alone.

I took him outside in the back yard where we could be alone and explained to him as best as I could that the matter was serious.

"I need to ask you again, did the church youth worker try to molest you?"

He replied, "Yes, ma'am" and dropped his head down in shame.

I asked him why he didn't say yes when I asked him earlier. He explained that he was too embarrassed, for fear others would make fun of him.

Oh God! Oh my God! It was more than I could bear when he answered yes. "I can't bear this Lord!" I thought. "I can't - not another one of my sons." I don't know how I responded to him. I took off running and screaming! This man wanted to destroy my sons - my babies. I stopped screaming and then wept until my weeping ran dry. I wept because my son was so innocent. I wept because he was such a child. I wept because I saw him and his brother and realized this pedophile took advantage of my family. I stopped crying long enough to call the elder again and repeat the event to her on the phone. She came running, as did my pastor and my son's Godfather.

This time we waited at my house for the police to arrive to make another report. It was much to bear to wait for hours. I began to weep again. This time I wept and crawled on my floor like an animal. I wept like a woman in labor whose pain consumed her. I wept in the arms of an elder who kept saying, "Darla, you can't lose your mind, not today my sister. You have to fight for your children." She kept reminding me that they had no one to fight for them but me. She kept reminding me that this was present evil coming against my family and it had to be destroyed. Over and over she told me that light is stronger than darkness and that I could bear this unbearable hurt and betrayal. I told her I couldn't, but she kept saying, "You can with the Restorer's help."

She didn't make excuses for why this happened. As a matter of fact, she said she had no answer for why it had happened. She promised God would be faithful and that He would give me the strength to fight and gain His victory. I could not blame God for all of this. I continue to believe, and know, that He is a sovereign God. That, for whatever reason, bad situations really do happen to good people.

My pastor's presence made a difference. He brought strength to my family - he stood as both pastor and protector. He prayed, not the church prayer, but the personal, individual prayer for us. He touched us and reassured us as he waited with us. He listened as the report was taken. He watched over my children and he talked with the police for them.

Can you imagine what it was like waiting for the police to arrive? It was painfully long and thoughts came to torment me as I waited: Thoughts of failure and hopelessness accompanied visions of what happened to my children. The voices around me continued to reassure me and kept me in reality so I could not slip into madness.

The police had the report and my pastor expressed some deep concerns about this pedophile that had keys to our church. He asked when we could possibly obtain an arrest. They assured us that they were going to get this information to a detective the following morning. They left me with a number to call first thing in the morning.

Everyone left that night and went home and I was alone with my children in the darkness - unknowing what tomorrow would bring. I didn't sleep. I didn't talk. I listened as my children slept through the night. I listened to their silent sleeping. I listened for the sound of any threat. I listened.

My mind continued to drift from place to place, like a ship in search of a safe harbor. I went back to that familiar Scripture of 1 Samuel 30, recalling that both of David's wives were kidnapped: one the mother of his first-born, or his strength, and the other representing his wisdom. I wondered how he agonized, and if his agony was the same as mine. What was his plan of recovery and could I recover my losses also? There were so many fragmented questions going on in my shocked mind. Some things cannot not be undone; however, it may be possible to repair or recover from the capture. One thing about David - he didn't ignore or underestimate his enemy. He didn't assume that because he was king he was protected from catastrophes. What he did was keep an open relationship with God so he could seek wisdom and help when needed.

I called my employer to advise them I wouldn't be at work the next day. You see, most people, when they hear you have six children, expect you to sit at home collecting welfare. Well, not true. I had to work to support them. They were the main reason I was trying not to lose my mind - because I was responsible for them. I contacted the detective next. She informed me the earliest she could possibly see me was in three weeks.

"Three weeks!" I exclaimed. "I can't wait three weeks. This man is always around children, and he has the keys to our church."

"I am sorry but that is the earliest we can get you in," she said.

My son's Godfather had been around our family for years. I told him what the detective said, and he responded quickly, agreeing with me that a quick resolution was necessary to get this pedophile arrested and away from other children. He called a family member, who happens to be the Chief of Police, and briefed him. In the meantime I called my pastor and told him what the detective said. He was outraged, suggesting that perhaps we should hire a private investigator to prove that this guy is a pedophile. Calling my children's Godfather seemed to have worked. An hour later I received a phone call to bring my children that afternoon to the Child Agency.

We finally arrived at the Child Agency for the interview with the detectives. I can't say that I arrived with any great expectations. I went because the authorities told me this was the next step in the process - a process that was taking over my life, and the lives of my children. I prepared myself as best as I could to answer questions and repeat the events over and over. I tried to deaden my reactions so I could at least be articulate. However, to my surprise, when I walked into the lobby, I found the receptionist and other staff members most sensitive to what has happened to my children. There were no accusations, no defense that I had to put up, no one wanting to persecute me. Rather, just folks who wanted to get the pedophile arrested.

"Have a seat, Ms Gooden. I'll let the detectives know that you are here."

"Ms. Gooden. Hi, we are the detectives that will be working your case. Are these your sons?"

"Yes," I replied.

"We are going to need them to come with us."

They guided my sons into a room with glass walls - a room parents were not allowed in, before they would take a report or ask for information. This room was filled with all kinds of scenes, park benches with ducks, video game areas, dollhouses, sports areas, music areas, and much more. Trees were painted along the floor and they "grew" all the way up to the ceilings. There were fountains and popcorn and it was a room for children to relax. I believe it was the beginning of the healing process - a place where they could again find the childhood they had been robbed of.

I could feel something different about this place as I watched my one son go to a computer, and the other son sprawl under a tree looking intently at the details in relaxation. This place was designed with him in mind. He looked, at that moment, the way he would have when this whole thing began - like someone caught in a time machine, his body growing but emotionally stunted. Rage burned in me again with its sharp turning blade and intensifying heat. I looked at his childhood they have been robbed of. Bitter tears filled my heart and found their way to my eyes. They were tears of regret, of loss, of anger, and, of course, betrayal. As I looked at the childlike lines across his face I wondered what kind of person could have done this, and how could they not only have fooled me, but so many other people at my church.

How did we all miss it? How did we not see the evil within him? We saw him all the time. He seemed so dedicated to his wife and son. He prayed in public, and this pedophile captured the hearts of many people with his childlike ways. His level of dedication to the youth was unmatched. Families invited him, his wife and his son into their home for fellowship. Other men sat and talked with him, sharing their own lives and families. They talked as men do about marriage, cars and sports. He loved music, especially gospel rap. He always drove his car playing it real loud and always was right there with the right song or ready to mix music with the children. He understood their language and was often found just sitting and talking to them about their future. He was always a part of some youth group or youth activity - not only at my own church but other churches in the area. How did we not see and why was it not revealed to us? There were so many questions that I didn't know to ask because, as far as I knew, my children were not in danger but were safe. As far as other parents knew their children were also safe and not in danger. If it takes a village to raise a child then a pedophile must betray the entire village to defile that child.

All these thoughts flooded my mind with just one look through the glass at a child safe for a moment, relaxing in a place made for him. The problem was this was not a real environment - it was one created to foster the feelings of safety and healing for wounded children. Our children don't live everyday behind glass walls in protected environments, they live out there in the now and nasty world where men of vile and unscrupulous motives set traps to steal their innocence and betray their confidences.

I waited for something to stir and for some miracle that didn't come. I waited for something normal in an abnormal situation. This was not my life - this was not supposed to happen to my children. I grew up in the church and took my children with me to church. They were involved in the activities of the church and in sports. I was trying hard to make a good life for them, working and providing a home in the Phoenix area. I worked hard to pay the mortgage and maintain it. I had six children to feed, to dress, do homework with, and oversee their lives - and I did it alone. I was not the happy and carefree divorcee that people write about, who spent all her time and money on herself. I know I didn't do everything right, but then I have never met parents who did. We have all made our own set of mistakes, and we should never forget them; it keeps us from being so judgmental with others. However, I did nothing to deserve this and, if this has happened in your family, neither did you.

I went to school conferences, reviewed the learning abilities of my children, and enrolled them in good recreational programs. I went to their sports games, plays, and spent time with their friends. I knew my neighbors and helped them when needed. I kept searching myself, blaming myself, listening to the whispers around me and I kept wondering if this was my fault. You see, part of the problem we face, or refuse to face, about pedophilia, it is part of a sub-culture. It is allowed to continue under a code of silence and shame. While we are standing still, accusing or excusing others or ourselves, the pedophile is stalking his next victim and taking advantage of our weaknesses. He is looking for the areas he can exploit, he knows that an unguarded city is easy to infiltrate.

He knows that rather than turn our attention upon him we will begin to bite and devour each other. He knows if he is discovered we will be in a state of shock and denial, affording him sufficient time to escape as we accuse one another. He knows we won't want to admit what has happened because we believe if we do, we have to admit failure. He knows that it isn't our failure but his nature taking the opportunity to satisfy the corrupt vileness in him.

That is what happened. My children were first betrayed and then violated. Then other children were betrayed and violated. Then parents who put their trust in people who faked genuineness were betrayed - the Christian community was betrayed, and even his family and friends were betrayed. The children were lured from their toy boxes into his depravity and into his indifference to satisfy his lewd and obscene habits under the false pretense of helping them. Betrayal, much like a local newspaper, continues to increase its circulation, and, like the common cold, it keeps spreading.

Eight

Throughout the ordeal, I often thought about David's situation: the enemy's attack affected not only his family but every family in the city. When the enemy came they didn't come to kill, they came to capture, transport and integrate the uncovered into their life style. That sounded very familiar to me, as David and his men wept until they had no strength. What a picture of loss, when the fighting men wept. When fighting men, were able to recognize that the loss of the wives, daughters, and sons, was of such significance, they wept until they were without strength. My whole being cried out for men of this caliber, who could grieve from the experience of loss and betrayal. Can you imagine men with breastplates, armor, swords and helmets losing their strength because of their families or their extended families? Before David could work on the solution, he and his men had to allow themselves to experience the loss affecting the entire city. At that point, I envied David because he was alone in his situation.

Seeing my son under that tree reminded me how alone he must have felt. You see, he didn't know there were others. The risk he took in disclosing what was done to him, he took alone with no supporting cast. You and I might know there was no risk in not being believed, but my son did not know. This pedophile distorted my son's views of what was happening and challenged even his family relationship in his efforts to isolate and keep my son captive for his use. When I thought about how alone he was, and how trapped by the uniqueness of this perversion, I was again filled with silent tears. They were silent now because I was standing proxy for the strong men who, as yet, had not responded to the loss.

The elder was with me so I could leave my sons for a moment to tell the detective the details of what they had told me. There were two white women detectives who interviewed my children. They were very firm in speech and physically fit for their career. They didn't want to hear much from me - not yet. All I could say were small details dealing with why I was there. They really wanted to talk to my boys - they needed more than me telling them what was told to me. Can you imagine trying to tell not only what happened to one son but trying to tell what happened to two? Just standing there, answering simple questions was a fight for control. They had to gently convince me to allow them access to my children. They needed to get this criminal arrested. "Okay, go ahead," I said, as they reassured me it was truly necessary. I took a deep breath and let them go, without me, to tell their story.

The elder and I sat like prisoners waiting for some type of release. Time, again, was agonizingly long. Trying to make conversation was pointless, so we sat together in the uncomfortable silence consoling one another with quick glances. I knew she wanted to tell me everything would be all right, but she thought better of it. Or, maybe she wanted to remind me of some of God's faithfulness in every situation. Instead, she chose to just sit with me in the valley so I would not be alone. Time is virtually immeasurable when you don't know what you are waiting for. I was just sitting on the outside of what they were saying, hoping they could convince someone that a crime had been committed. The waiting area was cheerful and bright with evidences of hope, so I tried to concentrate on them. It was a lot of work that forced my mind to be normal in an abnormal situation, so I just began to walk a little - going to the outside door and coming back. The elder stayed close enough to watch but far away enough not to intrude.

The door opened and one of my sons quickly passed me a quick look as he went back into the room with glass walls. It was becoming his retreat, he held me with his eyes and I held him back - yet I knew he needed the room. He needed his childhood back because reality was overwhelming. I watched him as he moved like an old man into the room that seemed to have transforming power - a room just for him, where he could, for a few moments, capture the world of a child. Wouldn't it be great if he could have just stayed in that room until all his wounds were healed? If he could have lay under the big tree and watched all the happy scenes of life and never have to face the *Big Nasty* again? I would have laid down right there with him and we could've talked about happier times and laughed. Unfortunately, we could not remember the happy days that day. That day was filled with too much pain and too much betrayal, that even the room could not heal.

My next son went in another room for his interview and I noted that although the same thing happened to both of them, their responses were different. I had so much to learn. I didn't understand that although it was the same person doing the same things, they were at different ages and one had just begun, while the other had been molested for a longer period of time. All this matters when dealing with responses, and it helps to understand that over a period of time the child's responses are dulled and the hope of release or help deadens. The pedophile begins with the child at a preadolescent stage, before he has any real exposure to his own sexuality.

It is easy to distort what you don't yet understand. The pedophile uses the absence of sexual understanding to distort the truth. It is not that our children don't have information - it is that they haven't yet felt or experienced sexual acts. They are innocent in their concept of sex, and this is the age that a pedophile seeks. It is not just a matter of age, but of innocence that he searches. Some children, by nature, are more curious than others about their own sexual nature. However, some are what we may call early or late bloomers. The pedophile looks for the not yet blooming - those become his targeted prey. Yes, I call them his prey because he seeks them out; he hunts them like an animal to look for their weaknesses to spoil them. He separates them from their families and exposes them to perversion.

Have you ever watched "Wild Kingdom" where animals stalk other animals? They look for the weak or the young to satisfy their hunger. They separate their prey from the herd and quickly pounce on them. This was the picture that was replayed in my mind - this animalistic method was used to criminally stalk and seek my children. He set some kind of a lure or net to catch them and then devoured them. "You can call me if you need anything." "I have movie passes if you want to go to the movies." "Would you be interested in going down to the studio and listening to some of our new artists?" "Do you have money for lunch or the latest outfits for school?" "I have the latest CD out for you to listen to." The more I thought over what they said - the more I watched them - the more I knew they had been exposed and stalked by a professional hunter.

Nine

It would take further input from my children before he could be captured. At the Child Agency the detectives who questioned my sons were more than convinced a crime had taken place. All of a sudden I saw more than just my anger. These professionals assured me this capture would take the highest priority. They specialized in sexual crimes against children and they knew the steps to take. I felt a bit of relief in seeing their anger and insistence; I needed someone to be angry with me. I needed someone to step in the fight with me. I had seen the anger of my pastor controlled because of my children, but then I saw the detectives as they began to map out a strategy for capture.

My children had to be medically examined. They were also given a blood test to ensure they had not been given any sexually transmitted disease. A what?! My mind tried to grasp this new thought - my babies given a disease? I had not even thought of that, but I guess it was possible. "Oh, God, oh no," I prayed, "not that, too!" I placed my hands over my head and stood there for a moment as I watched them go upstairs to the medical offices and my tears renewed themselves.

It was surprising how I could keep crying without even knowing it. Tears had a way of just slipping down my face without warning. They seemed to know when I needed to release some emotion to avoid explosion or implosion. I have come to respect tears as a way for the mind to release pain and, make no mistake about it, my mind was suffering real pain. It was locked in mortal combat, and tears were a bit of refreshing in mid-battle. What a relief when the physician informed me later that there were no diseases.

It was time to capture the predator. I remembered an illustration my pastor once gave about hunting a wolf. Older hunters would take a sharp knife and coat it in animal blood, freeze it and plant it in the ground. When the wolf found it, and he **would** find it, he would begin licking the blood and, in his passion for the blood, not notice when the blade cut his tongue. He continued licking it until he had lost so much blood that he was too weak to survive. The detectives asked one of my sons to put some blood on the blade, "Which one of you would be willing to get on the phone and assist in getting him to confess". We knew what this wolf craved, and we knew we would catch this wolf. We knew where he worked and where he lived, and we just needed to find out where he was without alerting him to the danger of capture.

When asked who could do this my younger son quickly said "I can do it". Wow! Their bravery still amazes me. My son got on the telephone and called the pedophile and engaged him in a confession of his acts against him. On tape, he admitted candidly what he had done to my son. I didn't want to hear the taping, and I wasn't allowed in the room while the call was being made, so my son could be natural and not try to protect me and be guarded in his conversation. Can you imagine the mixture of emotions I felt? He was so brave, and yet I feared that the predator would become suspicious and flee. Also I didn't want to ever expose him to his influence again. I was uncertain, but my son reassured me that he could do what was needed.

When later at trial, I heard the call on tape and marveled at the innocence of my son's questions. "Why did you hurt me"? "Why do you keep doing these things to me?" This pedophile promised that he wouldn't do it any more and apologized, "I am sorry, dog. I won't do it again, all right?" Then he quickly moved on to another subject like, "Where are you?" and "What's going on at home?" However, it was enough on tape to substantiate a verbal confession.

The detectives knew all his locations and addresses - my pastor had researched and found them. I gave the information to the detectives who refused to go home that night until they secured an arrest. It was a Friday night and I was concerned that if they didn't arrest him then he would either appear at church on Sunday, or he would possibly flee the state. I had a feeling he felt like we were on to him. The detectives assured me they would not go home to their own families until he was in jail and it would be before the night was over. Oh God... I couldn't tell if I felt relief or just weariness. It had been only a few days and, like Job 14:1 says, "They were full of trouble." They told me that my children and my job for that day were done and that we should go ahead and go home. The detectives said they would call as soon as the pedophile had been taken into custody.

Ten

Oh yes…the phone call came that same night. He was captured, arrested, and taken into custody. He was picked up at his second job. I thank God I had remembered where he worked. I am sure he was quite embarrassed as he was taken from there in handcuffs. But I didn't care - he needed to start feeling some shame for what he had done. This pedophile had filled the lives of my sons with such distortions and pain for self gratification. My boys would no longer have to face him again on the street or at church. We could finally begin the process of healing - if that was possible.

The Child Agency was scheduling therapy for my children to help them release and recover. I wanted the process to hurry and begin; somehow I thought this would soon be over. After all, he was arrested now. He had admitted his crime against both of my children later that night in a video with the detective. She did not coerce him - she just sat and listened as he disclosed information. Finally he said that he "felt so much better having the opportunity to get this all out so now he could move on with his life".

I was so relieved to know that it was finally over. However, relief really only comes that fast on television and not in real life. In real life there was so much time between the arrest and the actual trial. The detective said to me, "now that he is arrested, let's hope and pray that he takes the plea and spares the children a trial". I agreed.

I didn't know how my children's father would respond to the details of the abuse to his children. He was in a treatment program and I didn't want him to be overwhelmed, yet, I knew he needed to be informed. After almost seventeen years of balancing an unbalanced relationship and trying to keep the seesaw level, I knew I had to notify him.

We drove to the program where I was to tell him. He was cutting the hair of another resident, so I had to wait for him to finish. My life was like waiting at the emergency room and I was there but nothing got immediate attention. The sad part is I had gotten used to my issues coming last. So, I learned how to wait in patience. I told him the best I could, trying hard to remember every detail of importance. I didn't want to shut him out. He wanted to see them that night, so we drove over to my house and he cried with his children and hugged them and reassured them he would be there for them. He told them he loved them and they were important to him. Then I drove him back to the program and I waited for the next event.

Eleven

My concentration had been on my sons, I could not think beyond that point. However, with the arrest, my mind began to explore the possibility of more victims as something the detectives said about the pedophile's method not being the act of someone who was inexperienced registered in my subconscious.

He was not a beginner, or amateur, in his advances. Of course I had not yet considered him a career pedophile, but the thought of other children made me shudder. My thoughts went to other children I had seen him with and wondered what to do. I didn't know how to put out an "all points bulletin" for children who may have been molested. Maybe my children were really the only ones and this was a misconception on the part of the detectives. Yet, the thought of other children continued to haunt me, even though I was so weary in my own plight. At that moment I didn't have enough energy to pursue or fight for anyone else.

The job of the pastor is never done, and so in my absence he continued to pursue. How difficult it must have been for him to interview families, to explain what had happened and talk candidly to them about pedophilia. He wrote letters, made phone calls and contacted whomever he could to ensure everyone was notified of this youth leader's perversion. This pedophile was known through the valley as a gospel music rap artist, producer, and child mentor - not only in our church but in many other churches. I can't glamorize this person or his actions of sex crimes against children. His were well thought out plans to sexually molest and rob children of their identity and to destroy their futures.

When there is a crisis people will seek to blame someone for the occurrence. We have a tendency to want someone to pay or suffer for what has happened. David's men only responded to something or someone that they could possibly blame it on to feel better, knowing deep down inside that it wasn't their fault. That is the nature of our response to personal tragedy and crisis. The more

I kept looking at the situation with my children, the more I found myself initially pointing fingers - looking for someone else to blame, too:

- The pastor of the church - he allowed him to participate in ministry.
- The youth worker's wife - she should have been aware of what her husband was doing.
- The youth worker's friends - didn't they notice he was always with children?
- My ex-husband - he should have been in his place and not living a life on drugs, leaving his children unprotected.
- My son - why didn't he say something a lot sooner?
- The Youth Group Leaders - they did spend a lot of time in fellowship and not dealing with issues teens face.
- Finally myself - why didn't I see this about this person?

Yeah, myself. Why had I allowed him to have access to my children? I began to say what people around me were saying. The accusations, said in quiet tones, somehow got back to me. "You didn't see anything wrong or out of place?" "Don't you have 'mother's intuition'?" "Did you ever talk to your kids about good touch/bad touch?" They said I should have known better, that I put my children in danger - I should not have trusted anyone. They said, "You should have paid more attention," and, of course, it was me they blamed. They wanted to know where I was when all of this was going on. In turn, I was blaming them for not being available, for not helping, for not seeing, for letting this happen, too.

Yet, here was the pastor searching the congregation and notifying other pastors. This was not the job of weaklings, or those who wished to preserve their image. This was the immediate response of a team that moved in the midst of crisis to ensure the safety of those that remained to make sure others were not suffering in silence. In this process two more victims of this pedophile were discovered. When the news came from my pastor of other victims, I felt no sense of relief - only the sickening dread of someone else's pain. Because these acts were done to children, and the case was being made, every effort was made to protect their identity. They were given over to the detectives to be questioned as well. We couldn't even come together to console or mourn together. Each of us was alone with our torment, alone in our suffering and alone to find our solutions. This was when I first began to embrace the understanding of the power of fellowship in Jesus' suffering.

I was searching faces at first, wondering who it was until I realized everyone was searching my face, too. I didn't believe I would ever truly understand the why or how of it all. I only knew I would not tolerate, not for my children or for myself, shame for what we didn't do. I couldn't cringe in some secluded corner of life, ashamed or fearful. The future of my children required someone to fight and engage this enemy on their behalf. Every victim needs to know someone will fight for their cause.

I am not what some people would call strong, but I am a fighter. I have come to understand that when there is no man to provide support or cover, a woman must do what a woman must do. You don't get a lot of dinner invitations when you need to seat seven. People don't look forward to your visit with the children. My children, however, are my joy. My children are beautiful, well behaved, intelligent, and respectful. I am not continually at the principals' office or called to collect them for some disciplinary action. They are good children with innocent behavior patterns, and I wondered why **they** were hand picked by this predator. The only thing I could think of is their innocence had to be an attraction to this predator's criminal sexual appetite.

I wondered within myself if I should have prepared them for this by giving them all the gory details of sexual perversions. We had the talks about good and bad touching. We had not, however, discussed pedophilia. It was not a subject I had thought to discuss in detail. My children had been warned about strangers, but how do you warn them when the "stranger" is familiar and represents respected authority? How do you warn your sons about the pretense of love and the selfishness and perversion of men? How do you not sound out-dated or over-religious in a world that is so sexually casual and promiscuous and where almost anything goes?

The voice of the accuser tormented my mind with much guilt. What kind of parent would allow their children to go through this and not see anything? As if I was the kind of parent who would abuse my children, causing them to live in fear and pain, turning a deaf ear to their cries and pretending it is not happening. No, I took my children to church because I believe, and was raised to believe, this was where safety and love exists. However, while the church service was going on my sons had been sexually assaulted right in the midst of "Praise and Worship" in an upstairs closet!

I tried to make sense of something that just didn't make sense. No wonder David's men sought to kill him. I felt as though someone needed to pay. But the real truth was that the person who had done these acts needed to pay. Put the blame back where it belongs. Each one of David's men was bitter in spirit because of their sons and daughters and they wanted retribution. They knew someone should pay. After all, their families were too valuable to them. Can you imagine what it would have been like for Abigail and Ahinoam, plus the other women and children of David and his men, if no one sought them and if no one fought for them?

I have heard after years of suffering abused people become accustomed to the abuse. I didn't believe, or realize, how bad it was until it came to my attention. My sons brought abuse out into the open, not allowing it to hide in secret places. One of my sons had small changes in his behavior pattern that began to surface just prior to learning of the abuse. We can think our situation is normal or children are just adjusting, but we must dig real deep - deeper sometimes than we are comfortable digging. Abused children will cover themselves so the bruises or injuries don't show. It doesn't matter whether they are physical, mental or emotional. It doesn't matter how we try to hide our scars and bruises from those around us, at some point someone will notice or someone will cry out enough. As parents we must be willing to face the abuse and abuser, stop the insanity and not be content to put salve on it - giving our silent permission for the abuse to continue. Abusive lifestyles are not normal and tolerance for abuse can be passed from one generation to the next, so we must be careful what we teach our children to tolerate.

Twelve

Nothing is worse than finding out that someone you thought you knew never existed. I really thought this person was a good mentor, someone I could recommend to others - in fact I did. I recommended him to others just as he was recommended to me. If I had seen any hint of abnormal behavior, I would not have allowed him access to my children or anyone else's. Anyone who had any previous knowledge or experience with this pedophile became guilty with him by association if they failed to advise authorities or disallow him access to children. He came with references, so to speak, and the approval of authorities that I respected. What he offered my children he also offered others - it was a group of children and he was in the midst of them. That is why it didn't seem strange to me - not only was he interested in my children, he was interested and wanted to help all children - boys and girls. However, he seemed to be more drawn to the boys but no one really saw that until four victims later.

How did he have time to work, be married, be a father and molest four boys on a continual basis? I knew in my spirit there were more boys, but often times people are too ashamed because they are uninformed or their lives complicated with other issues keeping them from coming forward. Some of their responses to the unresolved issues relating to the molestation pushed them into negative behaviors that would make them seem incredulous or unbelievable.

The children were also uncertain after so much time had elapsed since the time it began. They were confused about their own participation. You see, this happened at such a vulnerable time in their emotional and sexual development, replacing the natural with the unnatural. We had to destroy the lies and communicate the truth; they had been robbed and deceived. More damages were done in the concealment of truth than in the revelation. These children needed to know they would be believed, avenged and that justice would work for them. They had to be reassured what happened to them was not their fault and it was criminally wrong. The lies they were told had to be destroyed by the power of positive love and truth. These terms had to be re-taught and correctly defined. Finally they could be free from the threats and fear they had been living with.

While writing this book, I was hoping more victims would surface, but not because I wanted or needed self-satisfaction. They needed to surface to know someone would believe them and fight for their voice to be heard. I wanted to mingle my tears with theirs, no matter how their lives had been affected by this crime. We could survive it together and overcome evil with good. We could overcome evil, not with a passive abstract good, but with the active and powerful good destroying the power of evil in their lives. I wanted to assure them of abundance of life after the unimaginable had occurred. And even if it had been cut down, the tree would blossom and live again. I wanted them to know even in the valley of great destruction, dead bones could arise and become an army of fighting men.

Thirteen

I heard the names of those boys representing the victims. Those boys were my boys - whether they were physically mine or not they were now all my boys. I heard over thirty counts of molestation against minors in one form or another. I wondered why outrage had not caused the judge's gavel to explode against his desk. How could we sit so quietly by and not scream in outrage at this atrocity? I knew if things held true to form, tears were about to be released as again and again I heard my children's names called out in a public courtroom. The court was not closed to visitors and anyone could have come, but many didn't. Anyone could have listened to the proceedings, even other predators. All privacy was vacated; so there in a public forum the charges were read.

I sat in the courtroom as the only parent next to my pastor. A few friends sat in seats behind me and I felt their strength. However, on the front row there was only my pastor, another youth worker and me. A representative from the advocates office was always somewhere nearby, explaining the process or reassuring me. I felt so old, but tried not to look it. I dressed that day with my children in mind. I knew they needed to see a fighter with all her wits working and not someone who was defeated. I had to be ready for the fight ahead, standing with them to join them in their battle unashamed. I would not allow them to wear someone else's shame because they had not done anything that warranted shame. I hoped their father would come and had notified him of the date, but in the end it was just the children and me.

The reading of the counts seemed to take forever and my children's names were mentioned repeatedly. I didn't know how they would react to them being read in the courtroom, for at this point they had no anonymity. I had chosen not to go for the jury selection and so this was my first time in court and seeing the jury. They were supposed to represent a polling of my peers, but I couldn't tell by looking at them if they would understand what had happened to my children or see some ethnic prototype. I wondered if they would relate to the crime against my children - this predator was such a manipulator. I hoped the case was well prepared so he didn't somehow slip through the cracks of our justice system. At every mention of the charges I flinched and looked over to see the all familiar clenching of my pastor's jaw. I knew this was rage under lock and key, and I was very familiar with it. We both sat stunned, awaiting the next stage of the trial to begin, which included the opening statement and the calling of the witnesses. My children and I were some of those witnesses.

Fourteen

How you begin life is vitally important. It can set the tone for your whole life. Many people have been born in a specific situation and have been stuck in that situation all their lives. How often we hear that our childhood experiences affect our adult lives. The things that happen to us affect us in the now and in the later. Regardless of how well adjusted we are, or how spiritual we are, we are affected by the things around us. Our ability to trust, our security, expectation, and social skills can be changed by positive or negative early life experiences.

It was amazing to hear presenting arguments on the same situations from different points of view. The prosecutor, attempting to show how heinous the crime was, and the defense attempting to convince the court it wasn't that bad. One side tried to prove criminal intent and the other side wanted the court to believe the pedophile was confused. I was not prepared for the defense because it enraged me to hear the attempt to defend or justify incomprehensible acts against children who could not defend themselves and therefore became victims.

How can you justify the molestation of a child? How do you ever make that right or natural? How can you defend the abuse of the helpless and innocent by one who plotted, schemed, and betrayed their trust? I didn't understand why this pedophile would want a trial, unless it was some additional perverted attack against the children - like a vampire desiring to extract the last ounce of life from them, or to use the trial as some type of conquest or trophy. Why else would he make them relive in a public court the acts he inflicted upon them, unless he derived pleasure from it? Yet, behind the purpose of a predator is a greater purpose to bring change through exposure. No one wants to be exposed, but without exposure there will never be change. Remember that this pedophile confessed to the detectives regarding my children and his lewd acts. It was the other two children he tried to deny, and that is what mandated this trial.

Did he think that people would understand or have sympathy for his actions? Did he somehow believe his own arguments that something in his life caused him to become a victim who now made victims of others? I knew this was an age-old battle of good against evil, it just seemed to me that good had gotten critically wounded in the battle and I wasn't sure if good would triumph. The courtroom was filled with the sounds of the impending fray as each attorney sharpened his sword before us. Could good really triumph over evil? Could darkness overcome light in this courtroom? These questions loomed large.

The opening remarks were filled with promised victories, setting the stage for all that would come. The attorneys were arrayed and suited up, each one fighting for his cause. I hoped that in the midst of the jousting my children's cause would not be forgotten. You see, my children desperately needed a visible champion - they needed to win. Due to the severity of the crimes, and yes they were crimes, these opponents came out with big swords in this judicial face off. They held them high over the court, each one hoping to enter the ring with a better advantage than his opponent. As much as I didn't want to be there, I knew I had to be, to resist evil and stand for my children.

We were well prepared by the advocate's office and had had the process explained to us. Yet, no matter how she explained it, my heart could not hold it. Carefully, and in detail, she outlined individually to my boys at their level of comprehension. I watched as she carefully touched and reassured them with gentle firmness. She spoke to each one alone, because even if the same thing happens to two people, the way they internalize and perceive it can be different. She separately explained it to me in big girl terms - not knowing I was a child, too. I was innocent in my ability to comprehend the process, and even though I remembered all she said, I was not prepared to be there.

During the proceedings I needed someone to help me maintain my sanity, and I was grateful for those who went with me. Even though I felt so alone, others continually reminded me that I was not alone. They pushed me pass the blank stare and forced me to communicate. You see, the problem was that the process isolated me from all that was normal. Their presence each day gave me strength and some sense of normality. I didn't hide from people - it only delayed my process, even though many didn't understand and some even hid from me.

I thank God that I had friends who stayed with me from the beginning, for it is not always easy to find those who will stand with you through the process because it takes so long. Most people desire you to hurry and get through it, or at least act like you have. They want you to hurry and get back to normal, as if the way things were was normal. What they meant was get back to the appearance of normal, and I refused to do that because it didn't resolve the crime and it didn't facilitate healing or empowerment. Find some friends, or let some friends find you. This is not something you should do alone. The nature of a crime like this will isolate you because there is so little knowledge about it and so much shame attached to it. People tend to shun away from what they don't understand - especially men. They fear and want to hide from it - or just hide it. We make it our own little nasty secret.

However, in this courtroom there would be no secrets, no private or hidden things. Everything would be disclosed and even the opening remarks would be graphic. I positioned myself with my feet squarely planted on the floor, hoping to maintain balance as the room began to spin. I could not even imagine being in the same room as this pedophile, and certainly not in such a small courtroom. In the movies the courtroom seems so big, but in real life you are within hearing distance of each other. I was afraid, not of my action, but of my children's reactions of having to face this perpetrator in this small room. It was not like the room at the Child Agency with encouragements placed thoughtfully about. This was a small, cold and vacant room. I wondered if any great amount of justice could be measured out in such a small room.

I searched the faces of the jurors who played an important role in the whole process. They decided if the case would be proved. The judge was honored, but he doesn't determine the guilt or innocence as he just presides over the court. I wondered about those jurors who held my children's lives in their hands - about their children, grandchildren, nieces and nephews. I hoped they understood "normal," and that was where their sympathies were. I looked at the judge and wondered if he would be just, or if this was just another case to him. You see, this involved my children - my greatest treasure - my heritage, and I desperately wanted some sign of outrage or vengeance.

I know God says, "Vengeance is mine" and that He will repay; yet, I hoped these people would be agents of His vengeance. Why would I not believe that God would desire vengeance and repayment? These actions were not what He determined for children. I wanted to see angels descending from heaven with their swords drawn to fight this evil and destroy it once and for all. I didn't want to see passivity and indifference in their faces, and I certainly didn't want to listen to the defense. With every word of defense a new wound opened fresh in my heart and my nails dug into my own flesh.

The lines between justice, judgment and vengeance are thin indeed. Judgment requires a payment. I understood this logic but it battled with my emotions that simply wanted to destroy this individual. I fought hard internal battles to get a grip on my emotions. I struggled to overcome the feelings of helplessness and bitterness, and in the process I came in contact with a very present evil. This evil tired and wearied me, yet my love for my children would not allow it to destroy them or me. I would not allow them to be held prisoner in an upside down world of sexual deviance and betrayal.

Part II
I OBJECT!

Fifteen

Suddenly the words of the prosecuting attorney began to hammer away at any attempt the defense would make. His arguments turned fierce and tension gripped the courtroom, transforming it from a spectator's box to battlefield. The attorneys stood behind small podiums to wage their warfare and they went at it like rock-um sock-um robots fighting in the mini ring. How could such powerful arguments come forward out of such a small platform, and how could justice be done in such a small space? In the end, who would lose their head? In this impassionate room, where these proceedings would play out, I began to understand the power of the tongue. The whole battle was one of words and wits as there was no forensic evidence of the crime perpetrated against the children. The prosecution had to make pictures with his words.

What we say really matters, and once a thing is said it cannot be taken back. No matter how we try to correct it we can't make the words not heard. So the words of these attorneys were put in the record, or recorded, and they were unchangeable. The case would be made by the presentation of the evidence in verbal argument. The case would be made by the words of witnesses who were children and who had been traumatized. Their words, my words, prosecuting words, defense words and finally the judge's words were the basis of the entire case.

All those words began to form an ever-tightening circle that enclosed my mind. I began to feel the intense pressure the words provoked. I wanted to run out of the courtroom, out into the street, and get lost in the crowds of nameless faces. I didn't want to sit in that small room that kept getting smaller and hear more and more of the vileness of this perpetrator and spoiler of children. Where was it that I could go to escape that moment? And if I was able to escape, what about my children? What about their future and their pain? If I stopped fighting for them, who would pick up their cause? No matter what I felt and how great this weight was upon me, I had to remember this happened to them.

Remember when I discussed earlier the night the call came after we left the detectives at the Child Agency? We had just arrived home and we were told that the pedophile had been arrested. There was no great celebration of the fact. We all sat silently around the table where we often talked. We hugged each other and kept asking each other if we were all right. And, of course, there were tears. It is hard to know what those tears were about - whether they were relief or regret. Whatever they were, they were not joyous. You see, we were still very much in that numbing shock that held us at a distance from the actual events. It wasn't that we were not aware of them; it was the news that reached us in muffled voices. Even when the detectives called and said "we got him" and, as they promised, they didn't go home until he was arrested - we were still numb.

Our elder sat with us and we all were quiet for some time. We reassured one another that we would be all right, and we touched each other to make sure we were still there. The silence in the house was unusual because with six children there are always voices and laughter - but this night there was unfamiliar silence. We didn't know what to expect and we didn't know how to comfort or encourage one another. It was an uncomfortable feeling of partial victory, with the absence of the anxiety of facing or seeing him again. Yet, we didn't experience the highly advertised closure. I remember one of my children asked, "But what will happen to him?"

On that night I had no response as to what would happen. As a matter of fact, I hoped he would burn in hell forever! I wanted revenge in the worst way imaginable. I was appalled at the question and thought, "why would he be concerned about what would happen to him after all that he had done". I didn't understand the process of pedophile enslavement and how it is used to keep the silence of the child. I was unable to help my child recover. I could not understand how he felt, but my motherly instinct spoke clearly to me to comfort my child and hold my anger. This was when I initially knew I needed information to help my children heal and that I felt so helpless and alone. This was also when I knew I needed to write this book to help others.

The innocence was still there and they did not yet understand the act of betrayal. You see, the methodology of the crime allows the pedophile to ingratiate himself in the lives of the children, and at a vulnerable stage of their development to confuse their loyalties and sense of right and wrong. This criminal appeared so accommodating, so sensitive to their needs and interested in their daily lives, while at the same time raping them. The pedophile convinces the child they are important to him and reassures them of their undivided attention so they begin to trust him. It is this trust that is then violated and betrayed. And it is this trust that must be carefully unmasked.

It is not just spending time with the child but it is learning how to reach that child. The pedophile spends time with children, learning what they respond to, not just his victims but all children. This one spent time with both boys and girls as he learned what they enjoyed. He spent time listening to their music, listening to their secrets and day-to-day activities and problems. He made himself an integral part of their daily lives. He understood their jokes and challenges. He shared their joys and encouraged them to believe they were the center of his world. He guarded their secrets and continued to pull them into a trusting relationship with him. You see, he first had to set the trap and make them comfortable in going in and out of the trap before he sprung it.

People will wonder why children seek attention from someone outside the family. Doesn't the family supply it? It is easier to believe that something is wrong with the family dynamics than it is to come to the realization that evil is always present, lurking and stalking. We don't have to live in fear of it, but we certainly should be aware of it. Our family is and was whole, just as normal as the family of anyone who reads this. Yes, we have our share of failures and are, perhaps, a bit dysfunctional - but whose family isn't? We love one another and have open avenues of communication. However, what you must know is the pedophile is a criminal with a deviant mind and behavior pattern. He looks for, and capitalizes, on every opportunity to become big brother, father or friend to all the children.

We put locks on our cars and houses to prevent theft, yet we know a good thief will find his way in. This is why, with all our locks and theft prevention, we also carry insurance. We plan to be safe and protect our homes; however we have theft, fire, flood, and acts of God insurance. Whatever is of value to us we insure to protect its value. We have all the warnings and information concerning drugs, and yet our communities are drug filled - not drug free, regardless of what signs we post.

The same is true with a pedophile - you can put up all the locks and alarms and still be victimized. Do we really believe that a car thief is craftier than a pedophile? We have to get rid of this outdated picture of some sleazy, obvious deviant in a raincoat with candy and recognize that the 21st century pedophile comes with iPods, sagging jeans, a good reputation, Bible in hand and the spirit of evil compromised in his heart.

Remember, I didn't meet this pedophile in a bar or out in the street. I wasn't some lonely woman, and we weren't in some illicit affair. He found his way into the everyday activities of my children. He found his way into the church, and patiently worked his way into an area of trust. He didn't have a prior arrest or conviction for crimes against children. He wasn't on drugs or involved in criminal activities. He was a college graduate, an articulate guy and a family man. He and his family were members of my church. He spent time with my children and his son spent time at my house with my children. He spoke continually of his faith and how he wanted to evangelize youth by helping them realize their potential. He was also a great listener and motivator.

It takes a lot of patience to stalk prey, and this pedophile was patient, observant, and watched for the smallest openings where children had a lack of confidence. He talked to the boys about girls and kept himself surrounded by girls to attract the boys. Like Paul says in the Bible in 1Corinthians 9:22, *he became all things to all men to win them.* Yeah, this predator even perverted the Scriptures to his advantage; it was all about him and his needs. Like a caged animal he spent his time watching and waiting for the opportunity to pounce on his prey.

His intention was to make victims of them. The activity of an adult making sexual contact with children cannot be romanticized. He sought out boys at the pre-adolescence stage who were at the awkward beginnings of sexual and social development. He looked for their confusion and awkwardness and sought those who were self-conscious. He didn't seek teens or those who already had evolved or integrated into a set social pattern. He looked for the novice, the outsider, the sheltered, and, yes, the uncovered. He sought those who had not been overly exposed and those who had a conscious. He was worse than a thief looking for an open window or a way inside. He had this insatiable hunger within himself for the spoiling of children.

Once again let me assure you that no matter where you live, whatever your financial situation, whom you know or how well you are known in your community, someone is watching and hoping for an opportunity to wrongfully take advantage of your children. This is the world we live in, filled with sexually explicit and sexually provoking advertisements, music, movies, dress and language. We have become accustomed, with the subtle influence of sexuality, with the "anything goes" mentality, and we are almost shock proof. We hear of atrocities against children and our reactions are little more than vague interest. We are reduced to putting pictures of children on milk cartons with the hope of them being found. Not a day goes by that we don't hear on the news of some horrendous crime against a child and hear it said that it is a sign of our times.

Pedophiles breed in this atmosphere of apathy and indifference. "As long as it isn't happening to my child it is just a sad state of affairs," is the thought process of many. When will we wake up and know this is not "an affair" - it is a criminal action and invasion in our community? And, we are all open to this type of activity through our passivity. I refuse to say pedophilia is an illness, because with illness there is sympathy, treatment and the hope of recovery. With pedophilia there isn't remorse and, in most cases, no admittance of the wrong done - only a regret at being discovered and interrupted. The pedophile possesses the child like a trophy or as their personal property. They are often referred to as "my boy" and they are kept close at hand. This constant attachment creates an atmosphere of control for the pedophile and keeps the child feeling helpless, confused, and controlled or in captivity.

The closeness that a pedophile maintains does not have anything to do with love, but with the fear of discovery. The child is kept close to avoid the possibility of exposure and to give the pedophile continuous access and control of the child. It also promotes a dependence upon the perpetrator and provides them the sense of power over their victims. The sexual appetite of the pedophile is as abnormal as the act itself. The action is also not a homosexual relationship, but is one that is sexually stimulated by a child. This perversion seeks power and satisfaction of their powerlessness by molesting and victimizing the pre-pubescent child.

This is present evil and is relentless and insatiable, without thought of consequence or effect. It is a primal instinct that will continue to seek a child, helpless and innocent, for his own pleasure. Nothing that a pedophile does is done in love - only manipulation and self-gratification. There isn't any proven method of recognized treatment to fix who they have become. However, some professionals believe if pedophiles are apprehended young in life as teens, since many have been abused themselves and implement appropriate pharmacology or cognitive therapy treatment plans, there may be some hope. Yet, there aren't any significant evidences or studies of successful treatment that prevent reoccurrence.

I am not attempting to come across as some expert on pedophilia treatment with all the current psychiatric information. What I am doing is obtaining whatever information I can to understand what has happened to my children. I have to come against evil well armed with faith and information. I am determined my sons will recover and overcome this influence of evil and destroy its ability to exert any power in their present or future lives. I am further determined to aid children and families experiencing this same horrendous crime to come out of the shadows and receive help in their recovery. The only way we can do this is to make as much information available as we possibly can.

I had to clearly articulate with my children and help them understand this was a crime against them and not some defining of their personage. They had to know although the culprit was incarcerated there was no medical or psychiatric evidence of a cure available. This individual was making a replacement pool of children, like a feeding chain, to keep a continual supply of fresh and new children to satisfy his perversion. My children had to be taught that they were not unique or special to the pedophile. He used and abused them because of their youth and inexperience. He raped their bodies and confused their minds and for this he will be incarcerated. I know this now, but that night quiet comfort was all I could provide.

In the courtroom, a different anger arose - one that was persistent and now armed with knowledge. I found myself behind the prosecuting attorney, pushing with my spirit for justice with him. I wanted to hear his every word and take them apart in my mind to allow the impact of what he was saying to reinforce my strength. You see, the argument by the prosecutor began to work for me. He was not just setting the tone for the evidence he would present, but he was a representative of the agency of justice that also reinforced the hopes of recovery for the victims.

Thinking back to David, I wondered if the people in his savagely attacked city had hope once they heard and saw David make a positive step toward active recovery of what had been lost. It wasn't enough for him to sit and sympathize with them - they needed a course of action. For a brief moment I felt the surge of empowering hope they must have felt when David stopped crying, put the ephod aside, picked up his weapon of warfare and called for the fighting men. Like the people of Ziklag, I saw more than a companion in my suffering; but I began to gather the words of victory and those words said, "Pursue: for thou shalt surely overtake them, and without fail recover all."

At that moment the prosecuting attorney began to postulate with a voice of firm surety that he **would** prove this man did these things. He would prove, without doubt, the commission of the crime. I heard in my spirit, "without fail, we shall recover all." I wanted to engrave those words upon my heart and then realized, by the pain dwelling there, they already were.

Sixteen

The opening arguments were completed and the fighters were back in their appropriate corners. The prosecutor on the left side, the defense on the right, and my children and I were somewhere in the middle. I had been cautioned regarding any outburst; for fear that they could adversely affect the proceeding. So there I was, like a spectator, fighting to hold my composure as the expert witnesses described in detail what I had lived with for the past year. These were not the ringside tickets I would have secured, and the bell rang again for more testimony to come forth. My life was out there in plain view of anyone who would want to listen. The ordeal of molestation was talked about in very clinical terms - and I had to listen without any emotion!

The experts in the psychological trauma surrounding abused children gave their testimony so the prosecutor could help the jurors to understand the long-term effects of the abuse. They didn't intend to scare me, however when long term effects are discussed, it is frightening to a parent. Can you imagine there are people who are experts on the effects of sexual abuse on our children? It is an actual occupation. My mind had difficulty at first wrapping itself around that fact. I was just like everyone else and my children were numbers on a violent crime statistic in someone's drawer. I used to see the article in the newspaper or on the news and never considered the work it took to recover from the abuse. I had no idea of the effects. I thought once it stopped we hugged each other and healed. I didn't consider there might be a recovery period and all recoveries are not the same.

We applauded the rescue as the Calvary came over the hill without considering this was only the first phase in a battle strategy to undo the effects of pedophilia activity and abuse. Just as the seduction or trapping of the child into the secrecy of pedophilia took time, so, too, does unraveling all the lies, fears, shame and betrayal. Lord, how I cried out for the quick fix! After all, I have six children I didn't have the time, support or expertise for a post-pedophilia convalescing period. Nothing else stopped because of this - not school; grades; social, physical or physiological development; employment; or financial obligations. And all that times six! I wasn't prepared for the recovery anymore than I was prepared for the crime.

Have you ever watched a hamster in its cage? Often times, there is a running wheel and the animal gets on the wheel to exercise - running while standing in place. I have always felt so sorry for the animal that is ever running and doesn't get anywhere. Instead, he just remains caged. Much of what happened during this year, as we awaited trial, felt like exercise while trapped and running in place. To counteract that feeling my whole family actually did start running. We participated in 5k races together and we ran at parks together. We had to find a way out of the cage into some forward motion. Since the media had exposed us, our lives were not that private and running put some distance between the act and the visibility we were experiencing.

Running became my screaming place. It was where I could exhaust myself until I could sleep and it was where I had a sense of accomplishment. My children and I trained to run. We ran for distance, for speed, for endurance, for sanity and we ran to stay connected to one another. We won medals and awards and scored high in the state competitions because we continued to run. We faced the crowd and ran - not away, but with our scars and with our pain.

We climbed mountains because we needed to get on top of the situations blocking us - and then we ran some more. My children didn't just run - they trained to run to know their limits and then to exceed them. They built up their confidences and they became champions in running and in life. The running and writing has helped us heal and accomplish something that bound us together. We ran because we could not stand still and we couldn't run away and become lost.

On the road to recovery, my sons had different responses. My older son just froze. He stopped progressing and pushing and stood still. He needed time to recover and needed help adjusting, because the abuse was over a prolonged period of time. He froze at the age he was when the abuse began. It was as if he needed help to get moving from the pre-teen age to now. Anyone looking at him would think from the outside he looked like he was fine. He wasn't fine or okay - he was standing, frozen, at a window outside his own life watching what was going on. Pulling him back and pushing him forward was a hard job. Helping him become a willing participant in his life again was my driving force. He wanted to just be very still and hidden until it all went away and I could not allow him to be victimized any longer. He couldn't now be free of the abuse and still captured by the effects.

My other son just pushed passed it - he was in the flight or fight mode. Like the little gingerbread man he was running as fast as he could and nothing could stop him His response was to just keep going - to be involved in everything. If he just kept moving it would be all right, just as if it never happened. It would be like a dream he woke up from and, after awhile, he couldn't even remember what it was. As long as he kept moving, the effects of the abuse couldn't touch him. He preferred escape rather than to face it. So my mission was to bring him to a slowing, but not a screeching halt, so he could experience the impact and begin to recover.

I found myself energizing one child and slowing the other down, but finding no place for my own despair. I found excuses to go to the van and just sit, because there I could be alone and not have to have the answers. There I could just sit and stare at nothing - praying God would motivate me to keep going. I would just take off and run a mile or two to exhaust my body as it raced with my mind. I found short cries were good medicine. I was standing in the debris left in my life by the evilness, and I had to make sense of what I didn't understand myself. One thing I knew for sure - what I don't confront today I **will** have to face the next, and my children deserved a brighter tomorrow.

Capture doesn't finalize the conviction and the conviction doesn't erase the action or the reaction. Children are amazing in their ability to disassociate themselves from the facts, and that is a survival response. However, survival isn't enough - it is only the starting place. There is more to life that just surviving the bad that has happened.

Experts agree there are limited resources established for boys who have been sexually abused. This has a lot to do with male stereotyping. Many boys or young men may not come forward and admit they have been abused because it is viewed as weakness or unmanly. The concept of being a man at all times takes over, so they take the punch and absorb the pain – similar to "play fighting" among children. The problem with this concept is reality. At some point, probably when least expected, children will react to the action of abuse against them. After all, just because the pain is ignored, the problem doesn't disappear. It isn't logical. If that worked, why not just ignore the symptoms of any major illness and wait for it to disappear.

The child who is in the victim stage responds with fear - fight or flight. This is how the mind copes with the assault and abuse. The mind finds a coping response to avoid break down or shut down. I thank God everyday for the coping responses in my children because it is part of the healing process. Many children, especially boys, respond with negative behavior patterns such as drug addictions, physical violence, sexual perversion, mental or nervous breakdowns and suicide. This coping response or method helps the child survive mentally, physically, physiologically and emotionally. It is of the utmost importance that our children survive and they should be commended for their survival. They should be commended for not just taking the punch and absorbing the pain, but for reacting later in life. They need to understand that they didn't terminate by one of these methods or the other; they endured until help arrived. They endured the struggle in their own minds, emotions and bodies until they could be rescued and then restored. Can you imagine how fearful this must have been, wanting to be rescued and yet unable to cry out for the help? It must have been like being buried alive and struggling in the darkness where no one can see. Silence isn't always golden. In this case, my children were trapped behind enemy lines, being forced and manipulated into submission to a power-hungry and perverted pedophile that was without a conscious. Can you imagine if David had gone through all the work necessary to rescue Ahinoam and Abigail, just to find they had self-destroyed while being help captive? I congratulate my sons that they survived, and I thank God He provided a method of escape so they could endure it.

Remember, my children were not semi-adults or even teens - they were children. When this started people still questioned why there wasn't a cry for help or why didn't they speak up. They didn't understand the method of entrapment and how it was targeted toward children. The guilt they experienced as children and the emotional confusion the abuser had them in is a trap. We forget they are children, with a child's logic and fears, and the pedophile is wiser and shrewder than the immature child. He manipulates their minds, their words, and confuses their sense of right and wrong. This is why, how and what a pedophile looks for in children. Pedophilia is not primarily a sexual crime like rape. It is a power struggle experience for someone who is without personal power or restraint. It is someone seeking who they can dominate and control.

Once a child has been captured, regardless of whether they are kept in some garage or in plain view, the pedophile continues to manipulate and subjugate them on a daily basis. The child lives in fear in a place of terror because while entrapped they are being continually persuaded because they are so loved. Over time, love for them becomes perverted and they are warned no one will ever accept or understand them. The amount of fear and shame they live with causes them to escape in their minds. I am not certain which is greater - the fear or the shame.

As a child did you ever come face to face with another child who wanted to fight you - a bully? You can have several responses to this situation. You can be in fear, fight, take flight or freeze. None of these responses is without consequence and are typical of children sensing danger or a threat. Children who are being abused have these same responses. They are in a state of shock, confusion and fear. Shock because the unimaginable has happened to them, and for most of them, they can't articulate or define what has happened. These are their first sexual experiences as the pedophile stimulates before he captivates.

The children are in a state of fear everyday for the entire period they are under the control of the pedophile. They fear the continued abuse, which after it was initiated, became all about the pedophile and not about the child. They fear physical death if they refuse to continue in the abuse. They fear for their families; because this is the threat of their abuser, and, of course, they fear exposure. Can you imagine in a child's mind how awful exposure would be? How awful it would be if their mother or siblings were killed? They are enduring to spare the life of their mother, or sister, or brother; they are front line soldiers. They freeze and stand still until it is over, or they take flight and run away - physically or in their minds.

As a parent I had to reestablish a safe environment to avoid aggressive behavior and tantrums, or any other manifestation of their attempt at fight, flight or freeze. I helped them regain a sense of personal control and order. The children began to have some regressive behaviors that included clinging, excessive sleeping or sleeplessness and loss of any recent developmental gains or abilities. Anger and blame were directed toward me, as my sons were sometimes unresponsive or avoidant. One of my sons said to me "This would not have happened if you did not introduce him to us". They also responded by being quiet or withdrawn, and sometimes they just would daydream or stare off with a glazed look, or appear robot-like. They needed time to react and readjust, and they needed me to be sensitive to what they needed.

I had to be careful not to over respond or mistake their responses as being oppositional or defiant behavior, even when they didn't respond to directives and instructions. They needed space and permission to be angry without me becoming defensive and without us having power struggles. Just like the expert witness stated, although they were alarming responses, they were normal attempts to cope, restore, organize and control, or reestablish some order and wholeness to their lives. My children had a right to be angry, disappointed or depressed, and I had to be the thermostat keeping their responses within the emergency normal scope. Like a pressure cooker, I was the release valve that allowed them to release without explosion.

I thank God everyday for the people around me that gave me the same allowance.

They allowed me anger without explanation and tears without a cover up. They listened to me say the same things over and over. They heard me as I questioned myself and blamed myself. They pulled me from the edge and carried me back inside where I would be safe. They continued to help me plan and activate a normal schedule for the achievement and advancement of my children. They picked them up from counseling when I couldn't get off from work in time. They cheered for their victories and stayed within the realm of a measurable and normal relationship with my children and me. They received my hate mail and didn't send it back. They guarded my privacy and kept me looking good for the sake of my children. They may have been few, but they were diligent and lived their faith in the sight of my children.

Seventeen

And, the flag is still standing! Have you ever watched one of those old war movies where men are being attacked and you think they will be utterly destroyed, but then you see the flag still waving in the aftermath of the battle? As my son walked what must have seemed like one of the longest miles ever taken to the witness stand, I watched his innocence unfold itself and knew the flag was still standing, in spite of the abuse he was still suffering. The aftermath left by the evil pedophilia creates havoc in the lives of children that is severe, and, yet, my son was still standing. He was standing to be a witness against all odds. With bravery he faced the man who deceived, betrayed and molested him to say, "You are guilty and I am no longer under your control!" Freedom is startling and has majesty of its own!

In order to be a witness one must come awfully close to the event. When we look at soldiers who have come through war we know they have not gone through it without effect. How can a child be comfortable in a courtroom talking about the abuse they have suffered? This was now public domain and there wasn't any level of comfort for those who were witnesses and must speak out. My children and I had spent so much time rebuilding and restoring ourselves as a family, and there we were in open court having to relive in front of strangers the personal details of the abuse.

As acquainted as I have become with tears - to know the pathway they travel and where they meet for fellowship - I also have that same familiarity with rage. Rage cannot be reasoned with, it must be put under lock and key. Rage must be forced to submit to reason. It must be subdued, forced to the ground, handcuffed and held prisoner. Rage is menacing, stalking and methodical. It arises quickly with deadly force and must be as quickly apprehended before releasing and emptying itself. Rage is counterproductive in a courtroom. The poet Langston Hughes may have known rivers - deep rivers, but I have known rage - strong, relentless, and driven.

Rage within me refused to comprehend why this pedophile didn't just accept the plea negotiations. Each count of the indictment held more than the 35 years he was offered. Why did he insist on a trial and make the children go through this again in public? I wanted to cover them, not in shame because shame had already been identified as an agent of destruction. We learned how to overcome it by meeting its challenge. We freed ourselves from the weight and bondage it held by breaking the code of silence. I wanted to cover their vulnerability and provide the protection and support I knew they needed.

He, this criminal, desired to put them on display as if they were his personal trophies to parade in the courtroom and my rage wanted to destroy him for that. Rage has a burning acidity – and tastes like an over abundance of hot sauce in your mouth that cannot be swallowed or erased easily. I remember going to the zoo and watching a tiger pace in his cage; the menacing look in his eyes dared me to let him out, dared me to stare too long at his eyes. There I was in the courtroom, pacing in my short cage - surveying all that was around me, daring them to let me out. I was keeping rage under, forcibly subduing it and redirecting its energy. I knew that I was holding it for the day when I could use it to dismantle the work of pedophilia in the lives of other children and their families - to help them come out from the silence and shame and become victorious over evil.

But rage would not aid my children in the courtroom, or in the recovery process. Although my children needed the validation of my anger to even begin the process of releasing theirs, it had to be seasoned with wisdom. Wisdom was needed to maintain my rage so it didn't provoke shame, causing them to revert into a psychological hiding place. This hiding place is where they masked and hid their feelings, a place of non-communication or, even worse, of denial. I thought, "How can they deny this atrocity happened?" It would be easy to create a mental world of escape and file this chapter in it. The problem with the hiding places of the mind is the children would never know when and how they will express themselves later in life.

As much as I didn't want to hear the details of the abuse of my children, I couldn't allow it to be a monster literally hidden under their beds. I couldn't allow it to have power over their lives. I had to endure listening to all the details of their abuse - and only as they were willing to pour it out. All of it never came out at one time - it came out in drips and spurts and never in a flood. I believe God in His mercy knew that it would overwhelm us, and so He guarded our psyche as He guards our lives. Now all the secrets were being disclosed, lies were being dismantled; the cloak of deception removed and the perversion was seen in its self-purposing and exploitation of children.

Jurors don't want to see rage because it appears to them that parents are out of control and unable to manage themselves and their children. Even though my children were the ones against who the crime was perpetrated, I had to maintain civility to not negatively impact the trial. Also, the defense may have been able to use it as a reason to say the jury was prejudiced by my actions or appearance. The last thing I wanted was a mistrial and to start the process over. So I had to cage the tiger, hold the rage and endure the suffering. Yeah, it was suffering to hear and replay mind videos of my children exposed to sexual perversion, physically hurt and manipulated. I needed a sparring partner for my rage and I looked over at my pastor, watched him again reset his jaw line, and position himself for the words we both dreaded hearing.

I felt more secure sitting between my sister and pastor, as they are both fighters. I was confident we would hold back any invasion, if needed, together. The three of us braced ourselves, as there wasn't a nice way to ask the questions that had to be asked in public. The act of pedophilia was done in secret, but my children and I had to testify in open. I was aware of those behind us, our second line of defense, and I was grateful people cared about my children and would stand behind them. I was grateful my children would know the strength of their support and the compassion of their understanding. I wanted us to rise up and tear this pedophile apart - limb by limb! Oh, God, how I understand what David meant when he said, "My tears have been my meat day and night, while they continually say unto me, where is thy God?" - Psalms 42:3.

Eighteen

If I thought somehow or another, my faith in God was not being tested during the ordeal of the trial, I was so wrong. I was constantly confronted by people saying they admired my strength, while assuming it was self-manufactured or that I was in need of nothing. It was not a self-manifestation of strength they saw - it was the fight of faith - continual and relentless. It was the age-old combat of good that must triumph over evil. I was locked in warfare and it would not release me until the battle was won and the children were free. I could not back down from this cause and from the fight that was brought to me - not one I sought for myself. I had been dragged, kicking and screaming, the whole way into the continual clash of the Titans and I could not back down.

No matter how I tried to soften the affects of what must be discussed, they would disrupt peace. I spent a year putting pieces into place. I laced the pieces of my children's lives together - carefully, with the help of ministers, psychologists, friends and family. I hope I tied together the tapestry of their lives with sufficient strength to withstand this public examination. Can you imagine what this must have felt like to them? It was like having a doctor give an annual exam in front of an audience. To everyone else it may have been a legal process, but to my children it was talking about the *Big Nasty* in front of strangers. I was watching what had been carefully worked on the wheel handled by strangers and I questioned if they could withstand yet another attack, this time from the defense. When the time came to leave this courtroom, I had no fond memories or desire to revisit there again. Yet, I knew I would probably come again and again, because I would be supporting others who had to face this dragon.

Their testimonies began with the simple questions, like, "what is your name?" and "how old are you?" I wondered within myself, "do they mean in years of living or experiences lived?" As I heard my younger son respond I couldn't help but slip into the place of denial again, the place where I just didn't believe this was happening to me and certainly not to my babies. I commanded the moans inside my soul to be silent and not sing the song of Rachel - at least not that day.

I sat there searching the face of my younger son - watching for danger signs of any kind. I sat in my running position - ready to pounce to their defense if they showed any signs of weakness. My feet were firmly planted, one a little ahead of the other, to give me leverage in case I needed to overthrow some force that would come against them. I sat with eyes glued on them, with my peripheral vision on the pedophile. He was sitting there intently looking at them as a cat watches a bird. His predatory instincts must have thought they would be too traumatized to be effective witnesses. Little did he know we had been dismantling and destroying his work for the last year.

I needed to see the expression in his eyes as he sat watching. I needed to see what my children were facing; I was screaming within - get my son out of here. "Oh, God, not again," was my hearts cry. "Don't allow them to faint, become confused or again experience the terror." Yet my outward expression was confident. "Yes, son, you can do this - you are my champion." How was I supposed to just sit there, as if they could endure this public examination? The courtroom seating provided the pedophile protection from direct view, and his face was turned from us. We were seated behind and he was in front. He was facing my younger son. Oh, God, he was facing my younger son. Oh, God, I could not endure this and I could not allow him to go through this. I was fighting in myself - I needed to see what danger they might face. Just then, as if on cue, the victim advocate touched my shoulder to add her support, so I was settled for the moment.

My younger son, however, had to face him. His facial expressions were exposed to all - the pedophile, jurors, judge, the attorneys, and everyone else in the courtroom. He had to face the court, and the fact that the criminal had immunity from stares was just not fair. I had hoped there would be more friendly faces they could look out to see, more people supporting and not judging them or me. I wished strong men were there who could validate them and give them a sense of courage. I was grateful for Pastor and their godfather because they represented unashamed manhood and were standing with, and for, them as they had always been. They taught them much about being boys who turned into men, and stood by them through this.

As men, my brother, their godfather & friend, and my pastor represented the men who stood to exonerate and clearly define manhood for my boys that day. My boys could see the pain in their eyes and knew their strength and determination not to separate themselves from them. They needed to identify with whole men and see acceptance and compassion in their eyes. They needed to know they would be received in the family of manhood again.

These men may never know the importance they played that day in the lives of my children. There may not have been many men to support them, yet what they had was genuine. I hoped their father would attend to strengthen & reassure them but he did not, not one day in all the days of the trial.

My sons could not be prepared for this confrontation and I screamed within me, "Why couldn't they be spared this?" It was these acts of continued bravery from my children that tugged so painfully upon my heart. It was the act of cowardly evil of the pedophile that continually enraged. There was nothing left to do but to continue to sit and listen as questions were asked of children that they had no right to have to know.

I momentarily retreated in my mind back to David and the anger and hostility he suffered from the fathers and husbands of those taken captive. There was an outrage in the camp among the men who stood up and challenged David's kingship. Even though some of them fainted along the way, at least they started out with David to recover their families. They might have been weak but they went at least part of the way with him. I miss men who take a stand, who do more than just wear the gang colors but do the warfare. I miss men who will go with women into the battle, even those who can't go all they way. If they just start it is a blessing to have them for part of the journey. When men are seen in their war clothes, carrying their weapons of warfare, staring death in the face to retrieve loved ones, ease and safety are felt in the camp. Without it there is only betrayal, abandonment and vulnerability permeating the atmosphere.

Now, I do not brag of men's strength and forget the work of the ministry provided by the presence of women. It is not a comparison - it is when we provide what we can, where we can, in support and defense we triumph. I would not have made it through this year without the support of my sisters who continually made themselves available to my family and me. The few that refused to let us go during this year, shared our pain, kept our confidences and prayed and stayed with us are irreplaceable. This crime, however, came against the manhood of boys and that is when the presence of men is essential. Can you imagine how the wives and children of David and his men felt when they saw the Amalikites fearfully preparing for warfare because the men of Ziklag were on their way?

The smell of war was in the air that day and rescue was eminent. What more did we have to lose before going to the fight. What would it take to provoke me, like David and the men of Ziklag, to recover all? When would my children know the safety and protection of their fathers and brothers? When would men of war answer their cries? I felt those behind us beginning to press with me into the war going on in the courtroom and I knew no matter who was there and who was not, we would battle that day until victory was secured.

Who would have expected my son to demonstrate such bravery as this at such a young age? When I looked into his face I saw nervousness, fear, anxiety, and still the embers of shame. God knows I tried so hard to erase the shame but it would take more time and right then, he had to tell his story. There were the witnesses, too, and they carried scars within themselves. I sat with them, night after night, putting bandages and salve on the open scars of their mind, esteem, and understanding. Now they had to tell the events as they happened, tell the story of what happened to them on the way to manhood by someone who was supposed to be a friend. They had to tell the details of sexual abuse and betrayal, they had to defend themselves against this pedophile for one last time.

They had to remember to unfreeze - come back from flight - stop fighting within and re-live this in the presence of people who were going to judge them. Yes, they were going to judge them - to determine if their account was credible, believable or matched up with other facts in the case. They were being judged on points of memory of the exact details, and not the facts or acts. They were challenged as to what time of day, where they were positioned in the house or whether they drove north or south. These questions were like mini missiles sent to unnerve them or challenge the validity of their account.

As my younger son sat on the stand I began to revisit my crying place, and tears again gathered at the pool for the all too familiar fellowship of suffering. It was amazing how many tears I could access on any given day. My tears were not those of great sobbing and high-pitched moans, no movie drama scenes that day. They were silent tears that slowly ran down my cheeks and formed a puddle just beneath my chin. I had become so accustomed to them and they had become just as accustomed to the contour of my face, that we just allowed each other space.

Nineteen

The prosecutor began his questions regarding the effect of the crime upon my family. He asked me about my life and there was much to tell. I was then, and am still, a hard-working woman who is the mother of six children. Many people hear of my six children and assume that I am on welfare or didn't finish high school and that I am in some way draining their tax dollars. So the prosecutor took time to erase any stereotypes in the mind of the jury. He underscored the confidence I had in the accused was valid because of his association with youth through so many churches in the valley. He made sure the jury understood it wasn't a lack of intelligence, laziness, or carelessness that this individual had access to my children. He had access to many children, he chose mine for a multitude of reasons. He chose mine because, like David, the men were not in the camp.

The prosecutor gave a detailed picture of a chameleon blending in with the church to hide his sinister motives. He hid behind a cloak of faith, like the Serpent in the Garden, as if his actions were innocent. He acted as if he belonged in the Garden and all the time he was beguiling Eve. His destroyer would be her son and my sons were standing to destroy this pedophile's work. The prosecutor wanted the jury to know my sons, their habits, our home life and certainly our faith life. He built a strong under-girding to help brace me for the attack the defense would rise in an attempt to discredit me. He would come to attack me in already wounded places to confuse, discredit, and manipulate me. He thought he would cause me to stumble from the repeated blows to my sense of guilt.

Yeah, he knew I had guilt - anytime something happens to your children you automatically think about what you could have done to prevent it. When they fall off their bikes you wonder if you took the training wheels off too soon. When they are struggling in school you think you should have spent more time with that homework assignment. When they have a basketball game and they scored low you think, "If I only had been there to cheer them on." When they get a cold you wonder if their coat is heavy enough. So, as mothers, we always are thinking we could have done more and blame ourselves for the outcomes. This defense attorney wanted to hang me up on a pole to display guilt and fault in letting this happen. However, I didn't cause his evilness - we were victims of it.

There was not much I could say for the contempt I felt for the defense attorney. It may not have been Christian, but it was real. There wasn't enough money in the world for me to defend a child molester. What could possibly be said about someone who molests four different boys in the same church and still wanted to say he was not guilty? How could I have possibly, after hearing of the repeated molestation of my children in graphic details by an adult married man with a son, not feel violated, betrayed, and abused myself? Yet, I had to keep my composure and continue to answer loaded questions which were attacking my children and me.

He was trying to use my testimony to validate his character by asking me if he had helped my boys in any way. That is like the spider asking the fly caught in its web is he comfortable. He asked if the defendant came to my house and picked up my children from church, and didn't his wife help them with their homework. Yeah, but look at the cost he extracted! He picked them up so he could be alone with them; he planned trips so he could be alone with them; he came to my house under the pretense of faking interest so he could be alone with them. Yes, he was interested in them - because he wanted to molest them and he went to great lengths to capture them.

Yeah, he even would come and talk with me about his son and ask advice. He would talk about his wife and family to get advice and receive sympathy. He talked about my children with such fake Christian interest and he understood how difficult it was for me as a single mom. He complimented me on how I was bringing them up and what fine children they all were. He had such compassion for my boys growing up without a father. He was a father himself and it was difficult for him being away from his son. His son lived with his biological mother in another state and would come during vacations for visits. One year his son came and stayed with him and his wife for the year. His son spent a lot of time with my children; they enjoyed each other's company. He always explained how his wife was ill and he was doing all he could to care for her. However, now in hindsight, how could he when children always surrounded him? He made himself sound like this rescuing angel, sent among us to help us all.

It wasn't just me that he beguiled. He masked his intentions to many parents at the church we attended, and many more in the valley. He was always in there promoting and in the midst of some Christian youth activity. He was a friend to all the children - the boys as well as the girls. His interest, however, was mainly with the boys; the girls were just bait to keep the boys interested. He visited the homes of many of the church children. He worked diligently among Christian youth workers, helping to create youth programs, which would instill Christian ethics and doctrines - while conducting his molestation on the side. He was the proverbial wolf in sheep's clothing. He didn't just prey upon small churches, like the one we attended, but he went in disguise to larger churches, where he attempted, I believe, to find bigger fields to ravage.

He was into the music of the youth generation and talked their language. He was articulate, well groomed and worked off and on at respectable jobs such as a bank. He was able to fool many people about his objectives. He was a rapper, but not the gangster type. No, he put Scriptures to music and rapped about faith and the power of God - all the time, without any remorse, he repeatedly raped young boys. He made friends with other young men and couples in the congregation, enjoying their company and, again, used them to validate his identity. Everything was planned so he could have access to the children. He wasn't some man who was under the influence of a mind-altering drug who raped them; no he methodically and intentionally set up a trap to attract young people for his own sexual perversion.

No matter how this defending attorney tried to make him sound, he was evil. I did not allow my testimony to become confusing. I was more set in the defense of my children than he was in defending the pedophile. He wanted to use against me that fact that at times I worked more than one job. Well, of course I did - I had six children and wasn't on welfare. I had to do all that I could to meet their needs. If I were a man working multiple jobs to support my family, people would commend me for the effort. This attorney wanted to make it sound as if my children were neglected and I was an absentee parent. No matter how many jobs I worked, I did homework with my children and was there with them every night. Very seldom was I "out being social." I am a young woman and people see me and assume I have a great social life, when all I do is work and care for my children.

My children and I attended church together because I wanted them to be youth of faith and morals. I taught Sunday school and participated in other activities of the church. I also cleaned the church twice a week with my children as I didn't receive child support, so their daily needs were being met by me through the jobs I worked alone, and those we worked together!

Our home was always open to children and anyone who needed a meal or a helping hand. I grew up in a family of six children and so family life is what I know. We went to church and participated in the church as children. My mother always had her hand out to help whoever she could and I learned Christian outreach from her. My mother went to college as an adult and obtained her bachelors degree, so I am a strong advocate for education. I have lived in the same community all my life and my children and I are known in that community. I went to college to become a substance abuse counselor because I wanted to help my husband and others who were addicted to drugs and alcohol.

There I was on the witness stand not as a witness but defending my life and how I raised my children. Defending myself and I didn't even have a traffic ticket! But I was defending myself against a pedophile. I was on the witness stand to defend what kind of parent I was and I was burning with anger because I felt like a victim myself. I was on the witness stand in front of all those people controlling the rage, betrayal and violation I felt. I was on the witness stand fighting a battle in myself not to scream and jump over the tables and physically take out the pain of my children on this person they called the defendant. How was it possible that he could ever be viewed as a defendant? It sounds so pitiful to call him the defendant. He wasn't a defendant, he was a pedophile - a spoiler and a molester of children - and he was not sick he was evil.

The defense attorney wanted to bring up all the details to paint a picture of a concerned individual who had a heart for children. He wanted to make him appear to be this kind and attentive individual who was simply misunderstood and was kind to the children. Good men don't molest children; good men don't betray their wives and children. How does a good man molest children and stay good? How does he continue to go to church, pray, read the Bible and molest children? How can he live a contradictory life, lying to his wife, to God and the church members and pastors, to parents and to the children themselves? How does he move from church to church leaving a trail of victims behind? What kind of person would be able to keep their sanity and still be so completely evil at the same time? The answer was the one that was seated at the table in front of me, protected by the law that was to protect my children. I remember telling the defense, "I didn't think anything was wrong for I know he is married."

Conquer and divide is the strategy of any enemy. If he can cause us to turn upon ourselves or God, he can create a separation. Then, in the confusion, he can slip in unnoticed. This game of cat and mouse the defense attorney played with me was contemptible, but I could not allow my anger or impatience show. I had to continue being examined in public for the defense of this pedophile who raped and betrayed my children. The indignation and rage continued to swell within me. I felt violated and betrayed all over again. The inequity of the situation was that I could not call him any names or use any expletives that were objectionable; meanwhile the whole trial was objectionable to me.

I kept tight reigns on my emotions, my expressions and my rage as I relived the violation of my children.

During the trial, I had visions of the acts he committed I had come to know from my children. To my dismay I discovered that he raped them in the church, in my home, at the shopping mall in the bathroom, at his mother's house and anywhere else he could. He raped them and secured their silence by telling them if they told he would kill me. They lived in a constant state of fear, confusion, shame and betrayal. He raped my children and then he went into the church and prayed. He raped them and then dubbed them a CD of their favorite music. He raped them and then picked them up for Christian youth class or camp where he was a teacher. He raped them and then went home and ate dinner with his wife. He raped them and then went to work at the bank. He raped them and then he sat down to eat at my table and the table of many other Christian families. He raped them and then made songs about the power of God. He raped them, not once, but over and over again for years and I can't get those pictures out of my head. He raped them and I was left to defend them and myself in an open court, because this pedophile raped them.

Twenty

It was very important that this pedophile be convicted of his crime no matter what it cost me and no matter what people thought of me. His conviction would release my children from the strong hold this type of crime has. They needed to be vindicated and found innocent as he was found guilty. They needed to know justice works for them and that evil is punished. These may be simple truths, yet they are important to the healing of the soul. Other children also needed to know that, as a society, we will not tolerate this crime against them. They needed to know it will be punished to the full extent of the law.

I was sure there were more victims just from the pattern laid in his methodology. He was always searching for replacement children. Yeah, replacement children, so when this group became too old, when they began to take on the appearance of men and not children, he would have a new group to replace them. I was sure of this because even during the trial young men from other states that he resided in came forward with their families speaking of the abuse they endured for years. They spoke of the conflicts they now have in their lives that are attributed to the molestation and abuse. They spoke of their inability to move forward in their lives, their own sexual confusion and rage.

This pedophile entrapped the boys at about the age of 10 and slowly gained their confidence. Then he introduced them to some type of behavior their parents would not allow and used their guilt to threaten exposure and manipulate them in keeping silent about what he was doing to them. He convinced them that he loved them and, because he loved them, this was an appropriate way of demonstrating his love. Innocent in their understanding and confused by mixed messages, children hear about alternative life styles and there acceptability, but they don't have sufficient knowledge to understand the difference between the two. They are held prisoner by guilt, fear, and ignorance. Children are always at that age breaking or testing the rules set for them, and with coaxing, they exceed boundaries that are set for their protection.

Many will say this can only happen when fathers are absent from the home, but many of our children live in the home with fathers who have clothes hanging in their closets, but are still absent from the daily lives of their children. The children pay for our lack of dedication to their lives when we are so caught up in the affairs of our careers or callings, or in "getting ahead" that our sons & daughters live in fatherless homes. All their activities, promotions and celebrations are with the one parent and dad makes a guest appearance on the special occasions for a photo op.

The pedophile makes a study of the family dynamics and looks for the weak places in the family structure to slip in. He is excited by the danger and control. He thinks himself smarter and loves being in your house as an invited guest, but all the while he is scheming how to seduce, molest, and spoil your house. He eats at your table and laughs at your jokes, but all the while he is planning how to attack and destroy your family. He makes friends with you because of your children or access to children and he has a secret desire to scheme and eventually molest your child or a child you know.

I had to keep these thoughts in my head to stay ahead of the cross examination of the defense attorney. I had to remember that while I was sitting in the hot seat of justice, children were being molested and were wide-eyed in disbelief, betrayal, while screaming in silence. I remembered it was someone just like the person sitting in the courtroom, someone everyone trusted and liked. I had to know that I was answering questions for thousands of parents who had no support system, who didn't come forward, and whose children never told them what happened to them on the way to manhood. I became angrier with each question as I thought about the plight of the children trapped in pedophilia who spend their entire childhood in sexual slavery. I thought of those who would never reach adulthood because of the perversion and brutality they endured. And even those who commit suicide, unable to reconcile what has happened to them or find peace in this world. At that point, I was internally screaming in silence!

"God, please help me make a difference by paving a path for other children and their parents to follow that leads out of pedophilia and into freedom. Please don't let this have happened to my children without victory over evil. God, please help me control the rage and grief that I feel even now."

As I looked out in the small courtroom I saw the face of a friend sitting forward, eyes set on me, I felt their encouragement and readiness to join me if needed, and I was strengthened by them. I saw my pastor soften his face to remind me he understood and a gentle nod of his head to indicate I should keep on going and not quit; and he had my back. I watched my sister search my face for any sign that she should attack. Although I felt alone I was assured I was not alone, others were there fighting with me and fighting for my children. I prayed my voice was steady and not timid, and yet not sarcastic and full of hate. I had to do this right for my children because they didn't deserve what happened to them and they had no David to fight for them.

This public testimony felt like an attack that I was under. Like David in his plight of Ziklag, I strengthened and encouraged myself in the Lord. It may seem strange to people that while my family was going through this horrendous ordeal I was being strengthened by the Lord. It is the earnest of the Christian relationship that we, in the midst of our pain, are consoled, comforted, encouraged and fueled by God. Our fingers don't point at Him as the author of our dilemma because we know who orchestrated this and who is to blame. I have learned to wait patiently upon the Lord for His deliverance and to surround myself with people who speak faith and not doubt; and who see more in me than I see in myself. They constantly provoked me to grow and push through the barriers that were in my way.

Like David, I had my share of those who just complained and blamed me for every thing that happened. They didn't say it directly, but how loudly they said it under their breath and between their words. They spoke with smug assurance that this couldn't happen to them because they were somehow better equipped or more watchful. It **DID** happen to them - they were just asleep or didn't pay attention to the predator in their midst. Or perhaps they weren't as concerned about my children as they were about theirs. The truth is they entertained him and he laughed at them just like he laughed at me. However, unlike David, I had those who continually reminded me of God's faithfulness to deliver the godly and execute righteous judgment to those who oppress His people, especially His children.

During this year of waiting for the trial it has been difficult to move forward, but I was determined my family would survive and overcome this crime. We were building ourselves individually and building up our bond as a family. My sons continued with therapy - when they wanted to go I sent them and when they didn't want to go I took them. I sat with them through some of their sessions and others I waited for them. Their godfather and my brother took them also, giving them the security of a male presence. They had to recover and stand, so now, on this stand, I had to evidence their wholeness and persevere; not becoming entrapped by emotions or words.

During this year I also endured many faces of the changing opinions and reactions of people around us. I would not allow anyone to forget this had happened and go off quietly to Happy Village, USA. No, I continued to confront the issue and although it wasn't popular or convenient to people, I pushed awareness and accountability. Many people wanted me to just move on - after all, he was behind bars - why couldn't I just let it go so we could move on with other issues? Well, maybe because they were my children. I couldn't just let it go as if what happened to them was insignificant, setting precedence for how they viewed themselves. I wondered why some of the men who were the closest to the pedophile were so uncomfortable around me and so uncaring about this assault of my children. I was, and I am, suspicious and I wondered, "Did they really know what he was all about and didn't warn us? Were they also coconspirators, or cut from the same cloth?" If so, I prayed they would take this warning and make changes in their lives!

I was on the witness stand and I was also in the event - it was a curious place to be. I was testifying under oath and I **AM** of truth, yet I could not give any commentary but, rather, could only answer the questions I was asked. Just like a cat in a cage I was on view but not allowed to roam free in the corridor of justice. I had questions that I wanted to ask, but there was no forum in this justice system that allowed me the opportunity to have my questions answered. I was being interrogated and forced to validate my actions and defend myself as a parent, while at the same time remember dates, times and miscellaneous facts that happened over a five-year period of time. Tell me, can you remember if you went to the store four years ago on July 4th and, if you can, which store was it? See my point?

I was exhausted, spent like a prizefighter and unsure of what the ramification of this witness response was. I was so glad for someone who could simply drive me home and deposit me on my doorstep. I fixed my face, hid my confusion, and lightened my step. I steadied my voice and tried to remember something in the day that was amusing as I walked through the door of my house where six wonderful children were waiting. They were searching my face to be sure I was okay. I had to force myself to be okay, because if I was okay, so were they. If not, they had no stability and would blame themselves. Children are like that - they blame themselves for whatever goes wrong. They were not to blame for this - not that day or any other day.

Twenty-one

My one child was quite different from the other one. He did not want anyone else in the courtroom but me. So the advocate politely asked all of the onlookers to leave. That left the advocate and me to sit on the front row. Called by the prosecutor to take the stand, he gave a quick glance backward as he moved uneasily forward and his eyes showed me the pain of the moment. This was the day he dreaded, the day he would face the one who molested him for years and stretch out his finger and say he is the one. This was my son who began this whole investigation, who stepped forward and said, "I want him to go to jail". This pedophile could have still been at large, still raping children and still stalking new victims had not my son stood up and risked everything to say what happened to him.

The criminal act of pedophilia for so long has hidden behind closed doors of shame and secrecy and children have grown up into adulthood with severe scars that follow them into every other relationship they have. They are never free of the bondage of shame and the terror of the assault. My son decided he wanted this person to go to jail; he decided when he didn't know there was anyone else this criminal had assaulted. My son thought he was the only one, so he took the bull by the horns and decided he would turn the tables, and instead of being the victim, he would be the victor.

We thought that when he stepped forward his identity would be protected and people would not know who he was. After all, he was a child. The way the newspaper articles were written, people were able to ascertain it was my family. The newspaper reporters, in an effort to obtain a story and not protect our children, drew a circle around my family and the church we attended. Adults began asking my children if it was them. They stopped by our house unannounced to ask questions - they said because they were concerned. Their concern was temporal, it only lasted for a moment and then it was back to the usual daily events.

This is how immune we have become as a society to crimes against children; we hear so much of it that we've become desensitized. It is a common item on the daily news and it becomes less of a crime and more of a commentary of the times we live. Our children never have a voice or see these criminals come to justice because justice takes a second seat to sensationalism. Often society wants to hear the details of the assault but they don't want to join in the battle to stop pedophilia. Our children need to see more than a lukewarm generation that is more prone to accept evil than to resist and overcome it.

So there my son sat among those that would judge if what he said really happened. He was older then and not the cute little 9 or ten year old so he was at the time of molestation; so he was challenged by the defense aggressively. He was challenged about times, events, places, people and what he could remember was important. In the midst of a crisis people remember different things because they are traumatized by the event they are experiencing. Time or the day of the week is less important to children than the event. Their days often are separated between school days and weekends. To ask them if this happened on March 12th doesn't mean anything to them. The trauma of the event may erase the time of day or the day of the week because they simply blot it out. It is the way they protect their mind. As the expert witnesses testified, children sometimes freeze which means time also freezes. They only know what happened and whether it happened a little or a lot. They know if it hurt and they know the rewards they received.

This is how a child's mind is manipulated and how they are controlled. The pedophile hurts them and then rewards them. They continually tell them they love them and keep them near most of the time. Children don't know that the reason they're kept near is to satisfy the needs of the pedophile and to keep others from knowing what they're doing. Pedophiles don't think like adults they think like children; they respond like children. This is the aftershock they live in and why it is necessary they learn to face the reality of the act and release the pain.

I once read about the bonsai trees - those miniature oriental trees. It is the art of dwarfing trees or plants and developing them into an aesthetically appealing shape by growing, pruning and training in containers according to prescribed techniques. The same technique is used by the pedophile - control the environment as much as possible so the child will become more accustomed to their sexual domination and they can be easily manipulated. This is what my son endured and what, for the last year, I have been trying to unravel. It has been mind control and now here he sits in front of this person who for so long exerted dominance over him and forced him into submission to his depravity.

My son sat in front of what may have seemed like the whole world to him, responding to questions about the continual abuse he endured. There were adult sexual terms that he didn't even know what they were and they had to be explained to him. You see, this pedophile altered his maturing process so some of the social and sexual experiences he may have had, he knew nothing about. The dates and normal struggles of sexual tension that happens among youth he hadn't experienced because this criminal kept him as much as possible away from normal behavior.

I wanted him to transform into a child again, answering questions as if he were eleven or twelve years old, because that is about when it began with him. I wanted to desperately run to him and put my arms around him and tell him Mommy was there - but there was no place in the courtroom for the emotional attention he needed. I was praying that he could hold up - that he could respond accurately to the questions being asked - that he didn't fold. I wished he didn't have to sit facing this pedophile, but that was what justice I demanded. I was angered again because the face of the pedophile was hidden from everyone in the courtroom except the judge and jury, but my son was not hidden from anyone. He was back in the water with the shark that attacked him; he was back facing someone who abused and threatened his life and the life of his family. He was facing the one who grabbed him and threw him down and then sexually abused him; and he was facing this terror again.

The prosecutor asked questions about the normal things of life - what he was interested in, school and sports. He was painting the picture of the average child. However, we as a society do not want to believe this could happen to the average child. We want to think there is some family problem that makes the children more vulnerable to this kind of assault. We don't want to believe this can happen in our families because we have two parent homes where both mom and dad are there. Yet, how many times do you see only one parent doing all the parenting in a two-parent home? When I go to my children's games I usually see the same parent all the time with the child, and they long ago stopped making excuses for why their spouse was not there. Many of our children come from single parent homes, regardless of how many parents live in the house!

Those questions made my son more comfortable, yet I knew that no matter how comfortable the prosecutor made him, the defense would aggressively examine him. My son's nervousness began to quiet itself, and he was able to talk more clearly about the things that happened to him. The calmness of those in the courtroom as they listened was unbearable to me. Why were they calm? Shouldn't they have been up in arms, ready to tear him limb from limb? Instead they were listening and writing notes in their jury pads. I was searching the faces of the jury to see if they had any reaction at all, and I could see only a listening posture. Occasionally one would look down or away and I hoped that was because they could not stand the thought of these actions against a child.

The prosecutor went through all the counts of the crime and made sure the dates and details were consistent with the original report. He lingered on some aspects of the crime to establish a pattern as was demonstrated by my other son's testimony. This pattern of attack and abuse would also be detailed in the testimony of the other children who would testify. There were four children who stood up against this criminal; four who admitted, "This happened to me, too", with the same method of attack, the same threat, the same promise of fame, and the same method of control. My son was as clear as he could be, and he fought to answer all the questions in the presence of the pedophile.

When the defense attorney stood up I gripped the courtroom bench. My eyes were glued to him and my ears held onto every word he said. He first tried to piggyback on the calm and innocence of the prosecutor's examination, but soon his ulterior motives came out. He was the defense attorney and his job was to get this pedophile off if he could. He was not gentle or merciful - he was aggressive and repeatedly asked questions trying to confuse a young man already confused. Yes, my son was confused because years of his life had been stolen. He had been dominated and forced into this sub-culture that he didn't even know existed. He, and our family, lived under the threat of violence. He was my hero as he sacrificed himself because he thought he was saving me.

So, just like everyone else I sat, although I was impatient, and listened as this lawyer who would make money off my pain, continue to inflict pain upon my son. I looked around for a moment at the advocate and regained my composure - it helped to know that I was not alone. I watched my son finally finish with the defense lawyer, and then the prosecutor who went back over the details to make sure the dates, times, and occurrences were in the right order for the sake of the jury. I watched my son slump down in his seat and then, with a great weariness, move slowly from the witness chair with his head hung down. I wanted, right then and there, to run to him, but I knew he had to make this trip from the witness stand for himself, as it was another experience of manhood he had to endure. I wondered if he knew how proud of him I was, and I tried to find his eyes but they were covered in shame and I knew we still had much work to undo what the trial did to him.

I bolstered myself up as soon as he was in reach and walked with him out of the courtroom. The advocate and I had to let him know that it went well and that he had done all that was expected of him. We reminded him of all the children that were now safe because he came forward. We told him he was an unsung hero and I promised him I would not stop fighting for the rights of children. I told him again I was sorry, and promised I would help other parents see what was going on before it went this far. I told him I loved him and that I was so proud of him. We walked out of that courthouse together - both of us a little older than when we went in and weary from the battle of the day.

Twenty-two

How can one defend such a heinous crime? What are the words that one could say to justify what they have done to children? Why even bother to give a response, why not just serve your time in silence? I wasn't even concerned about what he would say and how he would attempt to defend himself. There could not ever be any defense, yet this criminal would try to do just that - defend his actions.

His lawyer wanted to refute some of the things that were said - like the fact that he could not have molested children in the church while service was going on because of the location of the sound booth that he worked. He tried to say he didn't molest my son at his mother's house, yet the new owner testified under oath that he surprised the defendant when he unlocked the door to find him in there one day with a little boy. (This pedophile still had the keys to a sold, vacant house). Even though they were dressed, one could imagine what he was doing in a vacant house with a little boy.

He said that he kissed my son and it went too far and that it was consensual, but how does a child of about nine or ten years old give consent? He said that it was a love relationship, but if it was why be so secret about it? He said many things, but the truth kept overriding everything he said. I couldn't even imagine what he thought. It appeared as if he believed if he could present things about his childhood and things that happened to him it would justify his actions. Did he believe he was the only person in the world that had a misbalanced childhood?

What showed more than anything else was his arrogance, his pride and his lustful nature. How could he continuously molest four different boys on a weekly basis? He wanted the jurors to believe he didn't do it as much as was said, but the fact he did it at all was why he was on trial. He wanted the court to believe that his wife was sick (and she was) and that is what drove him to molest children. His logic made no sense. He wanted the court to believe he was working so many jobs and taking care of his wife that he didn't have time to molest these children; yet he admitted to having sex with them. He could not refute his own confession on tape, but he tried.

He laughed as if there was something funny going on in that courtroom. He was insulted when asked if he was a homosexual.

"No!" he blared, "I am not a homosexual."

"Yet you continued to have sex with male children?"

"Yeah, but it was because I loved them."

The more he spoke the more sure I became that evil really existed. It is not some figment of our imagination, but it is real and people who submit themselves to it are controlled by it. He was on the stand having his five minutes of fame and enjoying every moment of it.

I wondered why he didn't accept the plea bargain of thirty-five years rather than face the penalty for over thirty counts of child molestation and sexual contact with a minor. One of the young people who testified was past his teen years he denied that he had been molested. Yet I was sure he had because of the way it was done and the aggressiveness and the fear and contempt I saw in the young man's eyes as he testified. There were no witnesses to corroborate his story and no one to stand with him. My heart ached for him, as he was truly alone standing against a serial predator.

The pedophile wanted to talk about his music and how the children wanted to be a part of the music industry. He wanted to paint himself as some music mogul who was trying to help young people break into show business. Yet, with all that he was saying, he had no connections. He worked at a bank and part-time at a car rental agency - what did he possibly have to offer them? He was unemployed on a regular basis, constantly moving from one address to another. He moved in with his mother - so again, what did he have to offer? Once the mystique was removed, all that remained was a pedophile.

The prosecutor tore into him like a hungry bear just out of hibernation. He was relentless in his questions. He tore away all the lies and deceptions and showed the picture of a pedophile - one who stalks children and is aroused by their innocence and naivety - a person who watches those children, lurking around behind the back of their parents, under-minding them and drawing their children into a web of corruption. The prosecutor had no mercy in depicting him as what he was - a predator who was, and always would be, relentless in his pursuit of children to satisfy his evil desires. One who befriended people in the community, church, and persons who had access to children for the explicit purpose of molestation.

He took the mask of innocence off the pedophile and showed the entire court what he looked like - a hungry jackal seeking young prey to devour. A predator that used everyone he came in contact with to serve his lustful pleasures. A predator, without conscience, raped and threatened young boys for years - keeping them as prisoners of fear and shame. A predator who had no respect for his wife and who used her influence with children to give him credibility. A pedophile, made friends with Christian youth, pastors, and workers with his glibness and confession of faith, so he could access the children.

A pedophile that couldn't forsake his job because of the time he needed to stalk and trap children. He was a predator that took pictures of his victims and kept them in his secret stash place. A predator that was, even on the day he was arrested, talking to one of my children and admitting his sexual activity with them in a conversation being recorded by detectives. A predator that was busy online - always trying to find a new way to entice children. Oh, yeah, the mask was being taken off and yet this predator continued to smirk and make jokes that didn't make sense to anyone but him.

Many would say, "Oh, he was sick" but evil is not sickness. His actions were planned, premeditated and went on for years with some of the children. He was like a trained dog left in the house alone. He soiled everywhere he went. He had no repentance or sorrow for what he had done. He kept insisting it was consensual sex with a minor. **There is no such thing as consensual sex with a minor child, - it is illegal and immoral.** Yet, in his twisted reasoning, he found no problem with what he had done. He continued to blame every other situation or person in his life for his behavior. He blamed everyone except himself. He saw himself as some kind of father to the fatherless. He spoke of his faith, and yet his faith didn't stop him from child molestation.

There will always be bleeding hearts who want to see good in everyone, and I can give them their right to do so. However, I would warn them to keep their children behind safe doors if their hearts will bleed for this predator that, without mercy, preyed on young children. There are others who can say this is an illness that has no treatment or recovery at this time, but in time we may find a cure. I would respond, "Well, until there is a cure, the best we can do is incarcerate them without parole for as long as they live." If we don't, it is obvious they will continue to do the same thing. There is no remorse or sorrow; only betrayal and self-indulgence.

It wasn't sad to me that he had no one who stood for him, because he stood for no one but himself. He was in a constant state of deception and untruth, so when the prosecutor finally unmasked him, we all, for the first time, actually saw the real person beneath the mask. He was evil with all the connotations that evil has. He was cold, calculating, untrustworthy, self-centered, and sexually deviant. I sobbed because this was who had my children and I was unaware of who he was under the mask.

It was a day of silence because even those who came to support our families didn't expect to see such evil on display. They may have expected him to break down and confess, or sob and say he was sorry. But never in a million years did anyone expect he would, without conscience, admit to his crime and still expect to be found not guilty. He didn't believe himself that he was guilty of a crime, and that was evil personified. According to him, he was only doing what was right and satisfying to him, and the children just kept coming on to him and he could not resist them. He walked down from the stand as a man justified and not condemned by his actions. He walked away with a grim smile as if he had accomplished something great. He walked away believing in his heart that evil had triumphed over good, but oh how wrong he was!

Part III
THE VERDICT

Twenty-three

It is one thing to be tried by your peers, but in this case, who wants to be the peer of a pedophile? The jurors had to wait until after the holidays because the trial was going on during the Christmas Season. What a way to celebrate the birth of Christ - by exposing evil. It was a Christmas I will never forget. We waited with uncertainty; we waited to see what they would find. We had to go through the everyday living and holiday gift-giving, yet still have that anxiety of unfinished business in the back of our minds.

The holidays were over, it was the first of the year and we were back in court again. After the closing arguments were done we had to wait again. This time I kept asking the elder everyday as we waited, "Do you think they will find him guilty? Did the jury appear as though they believed the children?" What I found so interesting about the expert witness is she mentioned that sometimes girls might lie about being raped but boys rarely do.

"How many years do you think he will get?" I asked the elder.

She replied, "Well, Darla, I believe if he is found guilty on one count he'll probably be found guilty on all counts."

Wow! I thought. Then I started to feel sorry for this pedophile, and I had to tell myself, "No, Darla, don't feel sorry. He could have spared you and your family of this and he chose not to for over a year. The plea bargain of thirty-five years was on the table and at every hearing he declined it, even up until the time the trial began."

The phone call finally came - the verdict was in. I rushed downtown with the elder. I was so nervous and glad that the advocate met us on the outside of the courtroom. She briefly wanted to make sure that I was okay, and then told me it was time to go in. The jury walked in, followed by the Honorable Judge.

The Judge asked the jury, "Have you now reached a verdict?"

The response was "We have, your Honor."

I could have fainted. My palms were so sweaty. I thought to myself, "If he is found guilty this will really confirm that this did happen to my sons." The verdict was read. I heard my children's names then the sobs tore through my cracked throat. I could no longer hold back the moaning in my spirit. I heard my children's names being called over and over and over again and each time the woman juror said, "Guilty." I felt a knife being pressed into my heart. Twenty-five of the counts against him were sexual assault of my children and he was found guilty. I had nothing left within me. I had fought so hard to keep my composure and then all I could do was moan like a wounded animal. I cried again for the loss of the innocence of my children and the pain and fear they lived through; for this year of reproach and questioning by people who we believed would understand, or at the least be sympathetic; for the curious looks and less than quiet comments - made to them and about them; for the loneliness and separation they endured; for the sessions of therapy they went through to be able to withstand the trial.

I cried for all the nights I sat up listening to the details of what had happened to them; for the hours spent separating the lies from the truth; for the endless cleaning I did to purge my house; for the constant reminder a pedophile had intruded into the safety of my home; for the church services I attended when I wondered what this day would be like. I cried for all the families like mine who were enduring this rupture of their lives and who had to grieve in silence. People know what to do when someone dies or when they are sick, but they don't know what to do in this type of tragedy.

Some people spoke about celebrating. Though he was found guilty, nothing could ever cause me to celebrate. In that verdict was the pain and assault of my children. Someone foolishly said," Well now it is over and we can move on with our lives". I stared back with blank eyes. How do I move on as if what has happened to my children could be erased like chalk on a board? How do I press forward as if the past doesn't exist? These were the words of a fool - and an uncaring fool at that. This was an awful and tragic experience my son had on the way to manhood, and they, nor I, will ever forget it.

All I could hear that entire day was "guilty," and all I could do was cry. It became my pattern this crying. I had spent a year pushing my children, ministering to them, listening to them and comforting them. Now I was in need of help to recover from the betrayal and the act of violence done to me through the acts done to my children. I never checked to see the look on the defendant's face as I fled the courtroom that day as I couldn't see past the tears.

Twenty-four

I received a call that night from the District Attorney's Office asking me to speak to the press. What could I really say to the media? I struggled with the thought of making a public statement so I consulted with my children.

"How do you feel about me talking to the media about this case?" I asked. "Will you all be embarrassed"?

"No," they all replied.

Of course, being who they are, they wanted me to go forward. My daughter said, "Why should we carry his shame, we didn't do anything wrong?"

It is sad how much shame we bear, I remember that night being as tired as I was trying to prepare for the next day. I wondered what this was going to do to my family, friends, church members, pastors, neighbors and even the family of this pedophile. I didn't want to hurt anyone beyond where they were already hurt. Yet, I refused, as my daughter said, to wear the shame that wasn't mine. Coming out from behind the place of being silent and hidden took an extra amount of courage so I, like David, needed to call for the ephod to search myself and my motives. I felt the gentle push and reassurance that I needed to go forward and meet the press with the strength of the Lord preceding me.

My friend/sister drove down to the courthouse that morning and I remember my hands were so sweaty. I met first with the District Attorney and it was nice to know he also had children. After all, this was about children and their rights to be protected and not violated. He reassured me, and we agreed our children are so important if we are going to change society because they hold our future. We were both protecting the future of the city by standing for the children and their rights. As I looked over at my pastor, I saw the agreement we had concerning the children and felt his strength and passion for justice fueling me. He brought with him ministry updates to ensure the children were protected, even during the most sacred hour of the week, the hours we worship. We both felt the sadness of having to enforce protection - even in our churches. So he and I together, along with the District Attorney, went forward like pilgrims or sailors in uncharted waters to meet the press.

The District Attorney spoke first. He spoke about law and justice and the great victory for the rights of children. He thanked the prosecutor and all those who worked with such diligence for the children. As I looked around the room, bright lights glaring in my face, I thought of the faces of all those who the DA was alluding to - their tears, their encouragement - and I felt gratitude pushing me forward, because my story had become their story and my children their cause. Whether they wanted to or not, they had become infected and affected by what my children endured. I knew they would never be the same, and just as they were impacted, so should the community be impacted to stop the violence and betrayal of our children. The District Attorney further spoke about the severity of the sentence, speaking to those who would consider it an overkill of justice. He spoke of what cost would be too much for the life of a child. I wonder how valuable the children of the people who were sitting in that room were, and I wondered if they knew that this, too, could happen to them. I wondered how they would arm themselves and seek out justice beyond the measure of the law. It always seems like too much when you are on the outside looking in, but if it touches you and your children, your thinking will change.

Then it was my time to step up to the microphone. I remember being so nervous and so tired at the same time. It was a strange mixture of weariness, shock, fear, passion, and anxiety. Weariness because this was a yearlong battle of discovery, tears, treatment, exposure, and the constant opinions of others being thrown at me. I was like the salmon swimming upstream to give life to my children and I was weary, frail, and yet filled with the will to fight however needed for them. Shock because the sentence was given and the amount of time was incredible to me. Shock because no matter how much time he received, my children and I would never fully recover from the effects his violent attack left on us. I was shocked and stunned because the people who should have stood with me seemed to stand against me. Shock because I was alone and even their father refused to be a man of war for them. Fear because I had never stood in this place before - a place where literally millions would hear what I had to say as this broadcast went throughout the USA. I wanted to represent my children and their cause well and for people to know that so many children have, and are, suffering the same abuse. I wanted people to know that I was afraid because I am small, but then I remembered how big my God is and I stood in His strength.

My pastor spoke, giving a description of a corrupt individual filled with a desire for only self-satisfaction. He spoke of how the pedophile promised to make the children famous in the music industry through his connections. As a wolf was among the sheep, so was this predator among the sheep of his fold. He spoke of justice and his promise to ensure the children would recieve all the support they needed to recover. He spoke of our church making the changes to support the corrupt and fearless attack on children. He spoke of how our church was making charges to support the fight against this corrupt and fearless attack on children.

My voice was strong (so the people who saw the press conference said) but I did not feel it at the time. I felt inadequate, and unsure that others would understand my words. This was the press release that I gave on behalf of my children; they were the words I had to say to the USA. Wow! Even today, as I am writing this book, I am in awe of the method God used to make and force change…

I am standing today in an uncomfortable place. Somewhere I never imagined being. I am grieving. I am standing, as the voice of children, crying out to be freed from abuse and representing parents of children who have been and are being abused. You are not safe - **This can happen to you, too.** *Our Children are at risk in a society that is turning its back on them, and a deaf ear to their cries. These awful & nasty acts of abuse can happen even with people you trust. It can happen anywhere and with anyone - at school, at church, in community sponsored programs. It can happen, even with people you are supposed to be able to trust, so watch those who are entrusted with watching your children. We have to be aggressively on guard - asking specific questions of our children - looking for signs. Remember, your sons are at risk in this society as well as your daughters and they, too, need your protection. Predators are not what you think - they are common, regular people who appear trustworthy and come with references and validations.*

Remember, right now a child is being abused by someone they trust; even as you read this book, it is happening to some child… to some family… **right now!**

Remember, this can be happening in your house… today… by someone you trust … that seems to be kind hearted, with good intentions and <u>understanding</u>. Yet they are predators - watching for the opportunity to attack your sons…and your daughters.

Questions came from the media, one after the other, and I was surprised they wanted to know what I thought - as if I were some kind of expert on the subject of pedophilia. I continually use the word pedophilia because we cannot forget that this is what it was all about. It is not adult-child love, but the victimization of children - the rape and exploitation of them. These reporters stopped reporting for a moment and wanted to know what they could do to protect their children. I wanted their children safe, too, and gave as much moment-by-moment commentary as I could. If the people in this room were affected, how much more a nation that is continually, day-by-day, immune to the effects of pedophilia needed a wake up call and a trumpet to sound the alarm that we were being invaded and have been robbed. The questions were coming fast and just as fast, the answers seemed to pop right out of my mouth. I was so tired I couldn't even think - the impact of the secondary trauma had taken a toll on my mind. After a barrage of questions, the DA escorted me out and assured me that I had done a good job in communicating the cause. He felt it was a strong speech, but I was still just as exhausted.

I wanted to communicate that help is available, at least from me. I wanted to be an engine for change and help for children, parents, extended families, churches and communities who must no longer turn their eyes away, but must be ready to assist families who have been so victimized. The road to recovery begins with discovery, and the future can only be bright if light bearers are planted along the winding paths and the narrow dark alleys. I wasn't sure how I would become this engine for change, but one thing I knew was my life and the lives of my children had been forever changed and we refused to sit passively by and allow predators to victimize others.

The morning after the press conference my pastor contacted me to let me know that someone from another state had been looking for this defendant. She had seen the press conference on the Internet. After many months of searching for the defendant, the very day she typed his name to search for him the press conference appeared, so she sent an e-mail to our church. You see, the newspaper reports were good for something after all but God's timing was even better! My pastor placed a three-way phone call and she informed us that this same pedophile had come into her life. She said that there were two other young people who were also molested by this same pedophile in California, and one of them was her son. Their lives also reflected the havoc he authored. They were just children when it began, and he was once again in the church as a respected worker among the youth. Again, I remind you to watch those who watch your children. Not all youth workers are pedophiles - there are so many dedicated people who live their faith and are an asset in their care and responsible attitude toward children. There are, however, those far less dedicated and far more self-serving.

The boys she spoke of, now young men, had faced their molestation and betrayal without justice ever being served. Their church didn't stand with them and the order of the day was to just move on. The big cover up happened because no one wanted to deal with this *Big Nasty*. One of the boys had been hospitalized for severe mental disorders directly related to his molestation. The other has had much confusion and anger management issues. My pastor gave her information about our advocate and judge, hoping that she would at least write a letter if she couldn't make it to the sentencing. She said she would. However, I asked this mother if she would later that evening contact me with her son on the line. She said she would.

They called that evening and we talked for a very long time. For so many years he wanted to say something, but he said he just couldn't because of the shame. He then said that he wanted to come to the sentencing and he wanted to be there even if he could not speak. He and his mother wanted to witness his incarceration and, hopefully, get some closure. The dates were given and I prayed that they would be able to come.

Twenty-five

More than ever I was so proud of my children. I was so torn about doing the press conference, yet, had I not, we would not have found out about this other family. I knew first-hand the pain and guilt they had to endure. I got to talk to this mother over the phone, and at a later date over breakfast and lunch. It was as much for those boys that my boys sacrificed their anonymity and took the stand. It was for them, and so many more like them, that my son said "I want him to go to jail." It was for the pain and screams in the dark places that we don't even want to think about. It was the day the "boogieman" got his.

Days went by and we approached the time of the sentencing. I remember waking up that morning with knots in my stomach, uncertain of what the day would bring. I read in the newspapers that the defendant was facing up to 500 years. I received a phone call from that family from out of state and they had just arrived in town and were looking for a hotel room for the night. They found one nearby and I told them I would meet them the next morning for breakfast. It was still so unbelievable that this same molestation had happened to this young man in another state, and by this same pedophile who victimized my children. It was even more devastating to know that people knew about it at his former church and refused to prosecute him; leaving him free and able to molest my sons and others. I tried hard not to think of it too much, but sleep was far from me that night. I lie there with so many thoughts troubling me, so I called a friend and she listened as I once again poured my heart out. We need friends that will not get tired of listening to us as the infection is draining out of us.

I couldn't go back to sleep so I quickly dressed to meet them for breakfast. I couldn't believe my eyes when I saw the other victim; he was much taller than my son. He was a grown man, in his mid 20's, with children of his own. I knew he was uncomfortable at first because he kept moving around as we sat at the table. I understood because people judge and ask all the wrong questions. After introducing myself I sat down at the table. Mother to mother we talked and she began to warm up as we sat and talked.

She had told me how the defendant came into her life. She was a single mom herself, and the defendant was so helpful and quickly befriended her and her son. They all went to the same church for some time. One day she noticed after service their pastor was talking in a huddle with another family. She later found out that it was rumored that the defendant had molested another young man in the congregation. However, the incident was quickly hushed and the congregation was never informed of what had happened. It was said because of the relationship of the defendant's mother, who also attended the church, secrecy was kept. Through this conversation I found out there were more victims in other states. My mind began to scream, "Why hadn't anyone done anything?" There was no intervention for this child, and no warning for other parents to heed.

It appeared that for over twenty years this defendant had been involved in the sexual exploitation of young male children and had never been arrested or challenged. This mother asked her son, after she heard the rumors, about it and, of course, being young and in his early teens he denied it. This was appalling to me - that pastors responsible for the overseeing of the people would just avoid or withhold information that placed the children at risk. If accusations were made, even if they were unfounded, the least that should have been done was to ensure he had no future contact or relationship in the church with children. I could not understand this type of secrecy or reasoning. The silence and concealment, the lack of warning from the defendant's parents and prior pastors allowing this pedophile to continue and to even, by their negligence, hone his skills in stalking and securing children.

It wasn't until he became an adult that this young man finally told his mother. This was years before the trial, and she never had the opportunity to confront or prosecute this defendant. Now, with him facing 500 years, no one would invest in additional expenses to try him for the old case, since it would be out of Arizona jurisdiction and pointless to the legal system. I grieved for this young man who never had anyone to fight for his right and wept with him over his lost youth. I would have sat and listened and reassured him that this was a crime against him; just as I wept for those who were in the midst of abuse or who never told and struggle in solitude. This young man and his mother traveled at their own expense to seek whatever closure they could. They sent a letter prior to the sentencing to the judge. To some that may seem like a small thing, but after years of silence and brokenness, it was his voice screaming out against this molester.

It was time for me to move again, because it was the day of the sentencing and I was full of apprehension and exhaustion. Seeing that young man, however, strengthened me as I hoped it strengthened him and his family. We were one in the community of those who, like the Hurricane Katrina victims, were living in the results of a common event of destruction. It was a day full of many twists, turns and adjustments. Busy, and yet not too busy to stop and share time with someone else who had been wounded along the way. If I can say to you, as the community of people who know, take time to reach out in understanding or simple caring for the people you know are hurting. Your reaching out may be the beginning of their recovery, or, at the very least, will pull them out of loneliness, shame and isolation.

We made it downtown together. We got there, but I didn't know what to expect. There were six deputies in the courtroom that day - many more than had ever been there before. I kept trying to remind the young man from out of town to remain as calm as he possibly could, because this was an emotional day for him also. It had been years since he had seen the defendant, yet it seemed like yesterday in his pain. When the pedophile was ushered into the courtroom, I was surprised how much weight he had lost. This time he wasn't wearing regular clothes - he was wearing the uniform of a prisoner. After all, there was no jury to impress then. Some of the jurors sat in the audience, along with their families, as well as my fellow church members and friends. The jurors had connected with us through the suffering and pain my children endured.

We stood again as the judge entered the courtroom and they began to read off the charges. The prosecutor asked, on behalf of the pastor, if he could also make an impact statement but was denied by the judge. I slumped for a moment, wishing he could have spoken for us, too. The mother of the child who was also molested in this case with my children gave her impact statement first, and while she addressed the court I sat there watching with peripheral vision the face of the pedophile. There was still no remorse or sadness reflected. He sat there blankly staring at her, as behind me the out-of-town victim began to cry. The young man shifted his feet, and then he got up and stormed out of the courtroom. I wanted to run behind him to reassure, comfort and calm him, but I knew it was necessary for me to stay seated with my son. I had to be still because my children's impact statement would be next. Even though I hated being in that place, torn between the young man and my children, I had to weigh my every action.

It was just that quick and it was my turn to speak for my children. I was unsteady on my feet and my mind was not clear at all. It was not a good day for faltering, but I didn't have it together at all. One of my sons was there - my hero who refused to be silent any longer. Yeah, I came to court escorted by my hero son. He stepped out of his own comfort zone of invisibility, taking the risk to stand in the face of his molester. We were together, as we had been since the beginning, and he took his place behind me as I walked up to the podium as if to say, "Mama, this time I've got your back."

You see, I was his fighting tool and, like any good soldier, he stood behind his weapon. Isn't it amazing that as tired, confused, angry, weak, and disappointed as I was, and with a multitude of unresolved issues, I was to be the tool my son would use as his voice to speak what was in his heart that wouldn't, or just couldn't, come out? I will never forget how he stood behind me. Together he and I fought well that day. Every word I spoke to the judge he echoed in tears and sobs that could not be contained. He stood in agreement over every word I uttered, witnessing by his sobs the truth of it. It was if he continued to say "amen" over and over, but he only had tears, and I knew I was speaking his words. I felt him behind me, and again my retaliatory spirit rose - the fighting men had gone home from the battle and I was still there. I was there because he didn't deserve to have this happen to him. I was there because it wasn't enough for only justice to be served, but even in the face of this pedophile I had to curse the wrong and free the ones held captive by his dominance. I didn't want anyone to walk away that day unclear of what happened to my children and my entire family. I was not simply angry, I was driven - driven from within by the tears and sobs of my son standing behind me, and the children worldwide who had no voice and perhaps had lost hope. This will, and cannot, be tolerated, and I will never be quiet about the injustice and pain children suffer at the hands of evil and perverse men or women who prey upon them.

I reminded the judge this was a case of the continual rape and abuse of children and not the consensual sexual conduct we are so accustomed to in today's society. This was an act of criminal intent, and must be punished if our children are to sleep at night in peace. The eyes of the pedophile began to widen as if, finally, after all the legal proceeding, he began to realize the cost of his actions. I don't know what was going on in his head, but one thing I knew - my son and I held no punches - we stood our position as I read with deliberateness the impact statement. When I thought my strength was gone I heard a sob from behind me, from the pain of my son, and I knew then there was more to be said.

After I finished pouring out my words and sharing the impact this criminal had on my entire family in the presence of a judge with the responsibility of determining what course of punishment was right for the one who sat without remorse, I turned and hugged my son. With all the mother-power I had, I hugged him so he could feel the strength of my love and gratitude for allowing me to speak for him. I hugged him because we were one in that courtroom and because no matter how old he was he was my baby and I was so proud of his courage. As we stumbled to sit down the room was filled with emotional tears and embraces.

The room was quieted as the defending attorney spoke in an effort to reduce the amount of the pending sentencing. He argued no one could live long enough to serve the sentence. He further mentioned the defendant had been a victim of sexual abuse himself - as if that somehow could justify or give reason to his career of molesting children. Then the pedophile himself spoke, facing the judge. First he apologized to the pastor of our church, and I was appalled because it was the children he needed to apologize to first and last. Then he told me I had every right to be angry, as if I needed him to validate me or my feelings or responses. His arrogance was apparent to all who listened to his grandiose speaking. Finally he spoke of my children, who he said had a lot of courage and everything else he said became a blur to me. I was lost in the moment of even hearing this pedophile speak, after having seen his lack of remorse or sorrow.

Then, he abruptly turned around and told everyone he loved them. That was scary, because he also said he loved my children and look what he had done to them. He said "the church could use this," his molestation of children, "as a stepping stone to make us stronger". To the very end his arrogance and perversion would not allow him to have genuine remorse, nor did he have the ability to know or be impacted by the severity and wrongness of his actions. He stood there as if he were some perverted superhero, speaking words of encouragement to the troops as he went off sacrificially to the arena. I wasn't amazed, and was more certain that his punishment would fit his crimes against my children, and all the other children over the years of his career as a pedophile.

At that point, the judge spoke and his thoughts were precise and without mercy. They were the words that detailed betrayal at its highest level. He spoke of the rights of children to be protected and to live in a safe society. He spoke as a father; he spoke as a judge; he spoke as a victim's spokesman and he spoke with sternness and respect for the law. He had no mercy for one who showed no mercy - and that was a foundation I could understand. He didn't speak of vengeance, but he spoke of the protection for the innocent and the purpose of the law. He distributed justice with firmness, and he gave him every year that the counts dictated.

At the end I didn't celebrate over the 500-year sentence - nor did I call anyone. Instead, I went to lunch with my son and the family who came from out of town. The boys sat with each other, talking and encouraging one another. The mother and I sat silently - understanding. When we did speak, we spoke in general terms, but we didn't open any flood gates. I said goodbye to them as they left, knowing that they will always have a place in my heart.

Epilogue

As never before, life has taken on a whole new normal for me. I realize that even among the learned and influential of our communities, we need so much more in resources for our sons. More information must be made available, and parents need to have someone, and somewhere to turn.

I now feel so passionate about making myself available to speak whenever and wherever I can - at seminars, youth groups, parenting support groups, single's ministries and couple's awareness groups. I am happy to appear as a speaker or panel participant - providing resources and helping any way I can. I have dedicated myself to being available to help in the recovery and/or prevention process.

It is imperative that we don't assume once the perpetrator has been arrested all is well - your work with your children has just begun. Be ready for the occasional accusations, and remember you are still fighting for the wholeness of your child, so do not take it personally. Know that periodically, you will become the brunt of their frustrations, anger or even accusations. Just remember you are not the perpetrator. Nor the molester, nor the pedophile - you are the one in their life committed to their healing and wholeness. You are committed to their total recovery, which will take place little by little.

The recovery is a process and you will have days of success and days when you are overwhelmed by the aftermath. I felt like I needed to do something - and that something for me was to write a book and start a foundation for sexually abused boys and parents of the children abused. I have discovered there are limited agencies that address these issues of sexual abuse against boys. We are so familiar with the cause for girls, but the boys are left somewhere out there without covering and help. In Arizona there is very little group therapy for boys. How will they get the help that they need? How will families remain families without help and encouragement? How will communities, churches, and neighborhoods know what to look for, how to help, and how to prevent pedophilia from becoming an epidemic which, in my opinion, is totally out of control?

I needed help as I was falling apart on a daily basis. The question I faced was how could I give what I needed to others who may need it? Even when I went to parent meetings, I found people gravitating to me, wanting to know what to do and how to recover or discover. Everywhere I went there seemed to be someone who wanted me to listen to their story or, of course, a story about someone they knew. It is not a foreign experience in America for children to be victimized so it should not be so foreign for us to establish effective, local support and resource centers. There are so many parents who suffer in silence that need a voice and, sometimes more importantly, an ear.

In a society that promotes children's rights we must also make a greater effort to promote the rights of families to be united. We cannot help what we refuse to touch, talk about, or listen. Some of the behavior patterns we see in our children may have a root cause that we have not yet identified. Our "growing up talks" must include more information to be given and more to be gleaned. Whether our children's behavior is disruptive, abusive, addictive or changeable, the root cause must be investigated. Our children are individuals and their responses and reactions are individualized. Boys require as much development, time and resources as girls, and the shame of a boy violated must be eradicated. Rape and molestation, whether it is a boy or a girl, is a crime which should be prosecuted to the fullest extent of the law.

If I had to leave something for others to glean, or learn from my experiences, I would start with:

- Don't be arrogant enough to think this cannot happen to you or that your children are not at risk.
- I would say "No" more often and without a reason or without consideration of how that affects others. Saying "no" as a parent is also teaching your children to say "no."
- Have continual and repetitive talks about not only good and bad touching, but also clearly define terms that include bribery and seduction.
- Have suggestive talks that include dialogue, articles, music and role-playing, to help develop how to say no and how to be empowered.

Make no assumptions and don't be afraid to talk to other parents: Who you have entrusted with your children about how you feel, what you believe, and their accountability with your children.

- Remember pedophiles are where children are, so investigate people who are always surrounded by children to the excess - no matter what their title, position, or friendship.
- When your children want to talk, listen to what they say, and also how they say it. Listen closely to how they describe situations and people. Watch their behavior pattern.
- Remember - the pedophile will desensitize you to access your children. They will do this with compliments, interests, and even friendship.
- Remember that pedophiles are not old men in raincoats. They are contemporary, upwardly mobile, intelligent, married with children, and can be male or female.
- Don't be paranoid - but be informed and watchful.
- When you join a church, or go anywhere your children are entrusted to others, ask specific questions regarding how they qualify the people they hire or allow to be volunteers.
- Ask your pastor if he/she has any procedures in place to investigate, deter, and avoid child abuse. Also ask if there is any ongoing teaching regarding children at risk?
- Pastors need to find out what church new members previously attended, and what they were like as members.
- Develop a "family protection plan" that best suits your family. For example, as they reach an age where they can bathe themselves, teach them that when they take a bath, they take it alone. Allow your children to help you develop this "protection plan" - it is amazing the ideas that they come with that keeps them protected.

In conclusion, just let me say that in completing this book I felt that our ordeal was behind us. I knew there would still be a need for healing, which would, eventually, lead to complete closure. I assumed, however, that all the surprises had been sprung, that there was nothing else to discover or learn - and certainly nothing more to write about. Suffice it to say I was wrong, and what happened next has compelled me to write yet another book!